"Hall provides a wonderful exploration of a question at the heart of the biblical story—what does it look like for the world, and humanity, to be at rest?"

—Jon Collins, Cofounder
BibleProject

"Our contemporary culture has no idea what it means to experience the rest God intended. What's even more tragic is this—Christians have also lost their way. Gregory Hall invites us to rethink the meaning of 'Sabbath rest.' He rightly contends that God offers us something far beyond a lazy Sunday in a hammock. This book delivers a robust and fully developed biblical concept of the rest God intended for his children. The truths are not only profound, they are life-changing and full of grace."

—Morris Dirks, Founding Director
SoulFormation

"We live in a tired world. What people really need is a clear understanding of true rest. Hall offers this clarity by relating the Bible's ancient Near Eastern context to the biblical story. Then he helps us practically apply Jesus's offer of rest to our modern context. Many teachers write about sabbath today, but this work stands alone as truly unique in its approach and application."

—Chip Bennett, Lead Pastor
Grace Community Church, Sarasota, Florida

RETHINKING Rest

WHY OUR APPROACH TO SABBATH ISN'T WORKING

BY
GREGORY D. HALL

Deep River BOOKS

ISBN—13: 9781632695932
Library of Congress Control Number: 2022922902

Printed in the USA
2023—First Edition
31 30 29 28 27 26 25 24 23   10 9 8 7 6 5 4 3 2 1

CONTENTS

FOREWORD

What does it mean for God to "rest" (Genesis 2:2–3) and what does commandment four mean when it indicates that people should somehow be part of that "rest" (Exodus 20:8–11)? What did Sabbath observance require for the Israelites? Were the Jews of Jesus's time reading it correctly? How do Jesus's statements about the Sabbath enhance our understanding? What does Jesus mean when he offers to give "rest" (Matthew 11:28)? Should Christians be concerned about Sabbath observance today?

So many questions! These are all legitimate inquiries and concern interpretation of Scripture, understanding the ancient world, theological issues, and correlating Old Testament and New Testament, as well as considering modern appropriation and practice.

Some Christians have developed extreme lists of requirements for observing Sabbath; others happily dismiss it as part of the Law that should be considered obsolete. Stepping into this flurry of confusion, Gregory D. Hall here leads us through a careful and insightful study of the issues. He offers sure-handed guidance through the murky waters that so often bog us down as we seek to understand God's Word on this important and debated topic.

Combining the use of storytelling and careful textual work, Hall helps us to reevaluate many of the preconceptions about Sabbath that readers often have. In the process, he helps us reimagine what the Church is and does, and how we, as Christians, should understand our place in God's plans and purposes.

If Christians can absorb Hall's ideas and put them into practice, they will find themselves freed from the tyranny that their presuppositions have imposed on them. They will be able to appropriate the essential truth of what it means when God rests as well as to regain an understanding of the rest that God offers to his people and to which he calls them. I do not believe that I am overstating when I suggest that this book can revolutionize your thinking about God, the Bible, the Church, and your own relationship with God.

John H. Walton
Professor of Old Testament
Wheaton College

Additional Online Resources

RethinkingRest.com

At the beginning of each chapter, you'll see the "Additional Resources" QR code. This code links you to RethinkingRest.com, where you will find free companion resources for the *Rethinking Rest* book. These resources are available for individual and/or small group use.

Suggestions for Scripture Pre-Reading

Bible Lessons

Discussion Questions

Teaching Videos/Audio

Author's Q&R Forum

Suggestions for Additional Study

Electronic Endnotes

INTRODUCTION

I'm wondering why you picked up this book about "rest." Of all the subjects available, and all the things people are studying and learning these days, what caused you to open this one just now? What's going on in your life that brought you here?

Let me guess. You're tired.

You've got low energy.

Your motivation is not what it used to be, and before you go to the doctor and get a pill to fix it, you thought you'd read a . . .

(Sorry, now I'm projecting. Those are some of my issues.)

Whatever your reasoning, this book will challenge you to rethink your concept of rest. Would you expect anything less from something so titled? And your timing is exceptional, because "rethinking" seems to be in vogue. The information age is hurling unprecedented levels of previously unknown data at humanity at a blinding pace. This onslaught of information has caused us to reexamine many previously well-established conclusions. For instance, I grew up thinking Pluto was not only a lovable cartoon character but also a planet in our solar system. It's "new information" that has caused us to rethink some of our celestial assumptions.

Adam Grant, author of *Think Again: The Power of Knowing What You Don't Know,* suggests that the ability to rethink well-established ideas is an important skill set. But it's not always our favorite thing to do. There are deeply seated reasons behind our resistance to rethinking.

According to Grant, "we often prefer the ease of hanging on to old views over the difficulty of grappling with new ones. Yet there are also deeper forces behind our resistance to rethinking. Questioning ourselves makes the world more unpredictable. It requires us to admit that the facts may have changed, that what was once right may now be wrong. Reconsidering something we believe deeply can threaten our identities, making it feel as if we're losing a part of ourselves."[1]

This may be one reason why "new information" isn't always welcomed into the church. One might think, if God doesn't change, why would we need to rethink well-established ideas? But those committed to thoroughly understanding the Bible have always been willing to consider new information, and in the last hundred years much has been unearthed that's worthy of further study. The discovery of the Dead Sea Scrolls (1947–56) is but one example of "new information" within the last century that has given scholars much to rethink.

At the same time, it's important to remember that this process of discovery and consideration does not require one to abandon well-established theology. In his book *Old Testament Theology for Christians*, John H. Walton suggests, "Rethinking interpretation of a particular passage need not be viewed as undermining larger theological issues."[2]

In this book I will challenge you to reconsider several assumptions you may have regarding biblical rest. I'll ask you to expand your definitions to include things you may not have previously considered. But be assured, my purposes are not to undermine God's rest. I only wish to bring clarity to the topic.

Everyone seems to have well-established ideas of what rest is. There is even a culture war, between society and religion, to define the concept. But when pushed to clearly define the stuff of rest, it is often an exercise of smoke and mirrors. The harder we try to define rest, the less of it we all seem to have. This book will help change that. It will consider new information and give new categories to our data.

Grant points out the double standard society has regarding rethinking: "We laugh at people who still use Windows 95, yet we still cling to opinions that we formed in 1995. We listen to views that make us feel good, instead of ideas that make us think hard."[3] In regard to biblical rest, this book is all about the latter, and not so much the former.

I grew up playing baseball. There was a strong Little League tradition in our small Pacific Northwest community. One of the years I was in middle school (in the early 1980s), our local high-school baseball team made it to the playoffs. Most of the postseason games that year were played on weekdays after school, but the championship game happened to be scheduled for a Saturday afternoon. Normally this is a great idea. It allows teams and families time to travel and for the community to fully support their athletes.

That particular year, one of the best pitchers on the team (and his family) consistently observed a seventh-day sabbath. His family took Saturdays off from many of their normal weekday activities for religious purposes. As the team kept winning their playoff games, I remember there being great conversation in the community about whether the star pitcher would choose to play if they made it to the championship game. The team did keep winning, and they qualified to play that Saturday afternoon. After much discussion (and I'm assuming prayerful consideration as well), the pitcher decided to play in the title game. Even though they lost a close one-run contest that day, the conversation surrounding the decision to play, or not, made an early impact on my idea of the sabbath.

That baseball season was just a couple years after the movie *Chariots of Fire* won four Academy Awards (including Best Picture). For those who haven't seen it, *Chariots of Fire* is a film based on the true story of two British Olympic athletes in the 1924 games. One of the athletes, Eric Liddell, was favored to win the 100-meter race. Liddell was a devoutly religious man, and refused to run in a qualifying heat because it was held on Sunday.

Though I was young at the time, I remember being somewhat confused about how many different ideas and practices there were regarding this sacred concept. One athlete refuses to run on Sunday; another doesn't know if he should play baseball on Saturday. These ambiguities, and many others like them, have led to a general state of confusion for many. It's common for followers of Jesus to second-guess what the sabbath is and how they should respond to it.

Although rest is an ancient idea, it has found its way into modern culture in various forms. And it's not just for those that go to church anymore! Even secular society, lost somewhere between sleepless nights and chaotic schedules, has a somewhat romantic idea of what rest might mean. "Taking a sabbatical" has a nice ring to it. Some might think it's just another way to talk about a vacation. But few find the place where the roads cross, where the "theory of rest" meets the opportunity in life. If there were ever a time where resting was both countercultural and spiritually needed, it is now.

I think we can all agree that biblical rest is a confusing topic. It has been for me, and I don't think I'm alone. I grew up attending church, and one might think church attendance would bring more clarity, but it was in church that I found the greatest diversity regarding rest.

The author Rachel Held Evans suggests that the evangelical culture has failed to develop a robust theology of rest or of sabbath. And she is careful to separate "rest" and "sabbath," to stress the point that "all sabbath is rest, but not all rest is sabbath."[4]

Most within evangelicalism have assumed rest was simply one variation or another of observing the weekly sabbath (the fourth commandment). For years, that's what I assumed too.

My early confusion led to apathy and eventually, even though I remained a believer in Christ, I lost interest in the sabbath. It was later in life, while in my master's program, that I began to reengage with the topic. As I studied the book of Hebrews, I began to ask new questions about biblical rest. Those questions, and the answers that followed, led me to a surprising discovery, a greater understanding, and the desire to share my findings on this topic.

So to begin, let's ask these questions: What day is the sabbath? How do you interact with the concept of rest? How does rest influence your life on a weekly or even monthly basis?

I've asked many people these questions, and they've responded in dramatically different ways. Most of them fit into five similar categories that we will briefly discuss in the first chapter. My guess is that your response would fit into one of these categories as well. But this book isn't meant to settle arguments about what day the sabbath is, what activities are approved, or which ones should be avoided on such a day.

Rather, let's have a biblical discussion about godly rest. I propose we start at the beginning, Genesis, and hop and skip our way through the story of God and His creation. We will see that the idea of rest plays a surprisingly large and ever-expanding role in the overall biblical story. The mistake most of us make is when we allow our idea of large biblical concepts to develop out of just one or two Bible passages. Instead, we'll see that the context of each individual passage is really best understood from within a "forest for the trees" perspective. It's this broad context that will speak most loudly to much of the sabbath confusion.

In addition to examining the larger context of "rest," we will also try to answer some relevant questions you might be asking, like:

Why is it that God rested on the seventh day of creation? (I thought He was all-powerful.)

How is humanity's rest related to God's rest?

Is the sabbath always on a particular day of the week?

How does God define work?

Can someone piece together a sabbath experience in several short bursts throughout the week?

Does God expect believers today to practice sabbath?

How might all this relate to the ministry of Jesus and what He had to say about rest?

These are all good questions and we will discuss both theological and practical responses to each—and many more you probably haven't even considered yet.

Whatever your motivation is for reading this book, I'm guessing you wouldn't refuse if someone offered you a satisfying recipe for rest and a compelling argument to rethink what it means. The concepts I lay out in the following chapters have completely changed the way I approach biblical rest. Not only have my definitions changed, but so have the practical ways I pursue rest.

Biblical rest is a large part of God's story, but the church today is largely missing the breadth, depth, and beauty of Christ's easy yoke. So, no matter where you find yourself on the sabbath spectrum, I hope to awaken dormant interests, stretch established ideas, and bring new perspectives to the often-ignored offer of "biblical rest."

I invite you to turn the page and join me on the journey.

ADDITIONAL

REST

RESOURCES

CHAPTER 1

WHY RETHINK REST?

I don't know if you've noticed, but rest isn't working.

I'm not trying to say that the definition of rest is "not working." I mean: the concept of rest today is broken.

Humanity is a big group of tired people, and rest is proving to be more elusive than anyone ever imagined. As with most complex topics, people have come to very different conclusions about rest. Our ideas have become fractured and splintered to the point where most people don't really know what it is or how to get it. We are tired, and we have no idea how rest should interact with our exhaustion.

I'll use myself as an example. It seems like I'm tired most of the time. Sometimes I'm physically tired. At other times I'm mentally or emotionally exhausted—or all of these at once! I used to think that all I needed was a vacation. I often romanticized the idea. I was sure "the dream vacation" would include the ingredients to restore my soul. My wife Lisa and I would decide on a destination, negotiate the time off work, and buy the tickets. I imagined lying in a hammock under a palm tree on a beach somewhere.[5] I was sure that was where I would find rest.

But here's how my vacations usually play out: After getting to the destination, it takes me about two days to unhitch from regular life. About four days in, I start getting the uneasy feeling that I should be getting back home. When it actually is time to return, that "travel day" returning home is usually exhausting. After we arrive back, unpack, and get ready to head off to work, I often feel more tired than before I left.

Please tell me I'm not alone here!

That "vacation" idea of rest can't be the answer we're all looking for. It's so temporary. It's so fleeting. It's so *expensive!*

So, where else should we look to sort out the mess of our unrest?

Many look to the Bible to fix what is broken. You might be one of those. It's a good place to look, because the Bible has much to say about rest—it is first mentioned in the story of the creation in Genesis, and the idea is woven all through the Old and New Testaments. With all that the Bible offers regarding rest, I'd like to think those who regularly read the Bible would have better "rest success" than those who don't. But I don't think that's true. I think Christ-followers are often just as confused as everyone else.

Part of the problem is that we've truncated the idea. What do I mean? "Sabbath" is the word Bible-believers might use if pressed to define "rest." But the weekly sabbath is only a small subcategory of rest. Rest is a robust and fully developed biblical concept. Godly rest is so much more than the weekly sabbath.

We've Made the Sabbath into a Cul-de-sac Conversation

I think most people are familiar with the idea of a cul-de-sac. It's a type of street that dead-ends. It has a place to turn around, but it is not a through road. There's no exit other than going back from where you came.

We English speakers borrowed "cul-de-sac" from the French.[6] It's a term that literally means "the bottom of the bag." Like when you put your hand in a bag of potato chips and get to the bottom (because you've eaten all of them). You just got "cul-de-sac-ed" (that's not French; I just made that up) because there's no place to go but back to the top of the bag.

That's what sabbath conversations have become in the church today. They are cul-de-sac conversations. They don't have any outlets. Let me explain what I mean.

There are so many different ideas about what sabbath might be that people rarely get past a simple definition of the term. Most people think sabbath is really only about the fourth commandment,[7] but the fourth commandment is only a small sliver of what the Bible says about sabbath, and most churchgoers can't even agree what that commandment means. Following are some of the contemporary views based on interpretations of this commandment.

Friday Night to Saturday Night: We know the seventh-day sabbath in the Old Testament was a twenty-four-hour period of time beginning at sunset on Friday night. Some people in the church think Christians should return to a sabbath observance that mimics this Old Testament commandment.

Sunday's the Day: Some Bible readers notice in the New Testament that the church would gather on Sunday. These folks would argue that Saturday was the old covenant sabbath, but that Christians today are under a new covenant and that the example is to observe sabbath on Sunday.

Any Day . . . or Part of Any Day: Others think there's nothing special about one day over any other. They think God has given us more flexibility than that in the new covenant. They would say God doesn't really care what day it is. In fact, a Christian might even be able to piece-meal parts of days together throughout the week to fulfill the sabbath idea.

Christ Is the Sabbath: Others look at some of the statements that Jesus made regarding rest and conclude that the idea of sabbath is really just something that points to Jesus's ministry. But what does that even mean? While it sounds like a good "church answer," this type of view is really hard to pin down and seems to lack "boots on the ground" practicality.

Those are just some of the ways people pursue defining the sabbath.[8] Because of the diversity in opinions, our modern-day conversations have made the sabbath a theological cul-de-sac. We open up the topic, and we think we're heading down "Sabbath Street," but we get so caught up on how to even define the term that we find ourselves at the bottom of the bag with nowhere to go. People get stuck in debates about what day it should be observed, or what types of things people should be doing on those days. There's no exit out of those conversations; they don't lead anywhere else.

In reality, the topic of biblical rest is a neighborhood of highly interconnected streets. And when we are able to back away from our current cul-de-sac conversation and see the whole neighborhood of rest, that's when we can begin to understand what God means when He offers "rest."

I Don't Think That Means What You Think It Means

One of my favorite movies is the 1987 film *The Princess Bride*. Many of the actors from that film have gone on to have long and successful careers. For several of them, this was the film that propelled them forward. It is also a movie that has provided many memorable one-liners, like:

"People in masks cannot be trusted."[9]

"Never get involved in a land war in Asia."

"Mawwiage is what brings us together today."

Once, in a wedding I was officiating, I began the ceremony with this "mawwiage" line from the movie's wedding scene. It was received with a few isolated snickers in the audience, and a big smile from the groom. I enjoy trying to recite quotable movie lines in everyday circumstances, just to see who might notice.

One character in the movie, Vizzini, a "Sicilian man of genius," has a favorite word: "inconceivable." He says it quite often. In fact, he says it so often that he ends up using it in ways that are contrary to the word's meaning. At one point in the movie Vizzini thought he had killed the story's main character by cutting the rope he was utilizing to scale the

"Cliffs of Insanity." When Vizzini sees that his foe hasn't died, but is clinging to the side of the cliff, Vizzini uses his favorite word to describe the situation.

"Inconceivable!"

Another character, after having heard Vizzini use this word several times throughout the movie, responds, "You keep using that word. I do not think it means what you think it means."

I think some of us have gotten to exactly that point in our conversations about biblical rest. We use the term . . . but I don't think it means what we think it means. So let's get out of the cul-de-sac, come back to the Bible, and start at the beginning. I propose we build our perspective on the whole of the biblical narrative. We will see how the Bible begins with a creation at rest in Eden under God's rule and authority. We will see how that rest was disrupted and how God pursues His creation to reestablish restful rule.

The purpose of this study is to better understand biblical rest and to be able to negotiate the neighborhood well enough to arrive where God desires us all to land: in a place of true rest.

There Remains a Sabbath Rest

We could begin our trip through the biblical "neighborhood of rest" at the creation, in Genesis, and weave our way all the way through to the end of the story in Revelation. We will make our way back to Genesis soon enough, but I'd like to begin in the book of Hebrews. This is by design. There's a pivotal discussion in Hebrews 3–4 regarding the New Testament understanding of biblical rest. This discussion is unique because it directly connects the rest a believer experiences to the rest that God experiences. This connection is foundational if we are going to begin to rethink what rest is.

We are not going to look at that whole passage now. We're just going to begin using it as a base camp from which to start our journey. There's a specific passage in Hebrews 4 that will launch us back to the beginning of the story in Genesis.

Is sabbath rest really a concept on which modern believers need to focus? Let's consider what the author of Hebrews has to say:

> For if Joshua[10] had given them rest, He would not have spoken of another day after that. So there remains a Sabbath rest for the people of God. For the one who has entered His rest has himself also rested from his works, as God did from His. Therefore, let us be diligent to enter that rest. (Hebrews 4:8–11)

This passage mentions the Old Testament character of Joshua. Joshua was Moses's right-hand man. Moses led Israel out of Egypt, received the Ten Commandments, and led the people for a generation in the wilderness. Then Joshua went on to lead the Israelites into the land that God had promised to Israel's ancestor, Abraham. The Promised Land, into which Joshua led the conquest, is often referred to as a place of rest.

Hebrews 4:8 suggests that if Joshua had given the Israelites true rest (through the conquest of the Promised Land), He (God) would not have spoken of another day after the conquest, when the concept of rest was revisited.

There's something important to notice here. In maybe the most important conversation about biblical rest in the whole of the New Testament, we're talking about Joshua. But who are we *not* talking about?

Notice the absence of Moses in this discussion. Moses is the character most closely associated with the Old Testament rules about how to observe the weekly sabbath day. Yet the author of Hebrews doesn't go back and suggest that the fourth commandment was the defining path to sabbath rest. In fact, the author doesn't mention any part of the Mosaic Law in his argument. But that's where our cul-de-sac conversations are on this topic in church culture today. We go to the fourth commandment and get stuck there.

Instead, this Hebrews discussion talks about how *Joshua* wasn't able to offer the Israelites true rest. If the fourth commandment had been the end-all, it seems like we'd be reading about that here in Hebrews. But that's not where the argument takes us.

Hebrews 4:9 says, "So there remains a Sabbath rest for the people of God." It's important for modern readers to understand that we're not done with this topic yet. Or maybe better to say: God's not done with this topic.

Because of our sabbath confusion in the church, many people, including many in the next generation of church leaders, have completely abandoned the idea of sabbath. But God's not done with it. There is something about sabbath rest with which God expects believers to stay engaged. And maybe, sabbath doesn't mean what we think it means.

The next verse we need to look at is Hebrews 4:10: "For the one who has entered His rest has himself also rested from his works, as God did from His." It's important to pay attention to the capital letters in this verse; they refer to God.

Here's my own explanatory translation of what's going on. This passage is saying, "For the one [the believer in Christ] who has entered His rest [God's rest] has himself [the believer has] also rested from his works [the believer's own works], as God did from His [from God's work]."

It's a bit of a confusing statement, to be sure. To what is this even referring? When was it that God was working and then rested from His work?

Well, that's talking about the creation account in Genesis 1:1–2:3. This Hebrews passage is linking us back to Genesis. But notice where it's *not* sending us. It's not sending us back to the Ten Commandments in Exodus 20 or Deuteronomy 5. The answer isn't found there. The definition of rest existed well before the exodus from Egypt and before the Mosaic Law was ever written down. The author of Hebrews is suggesting that there's something unique about the Genesis creation account that holds the key to our understanding of rest.

Then in Hebrews 4:11, the author encourages us to "be diligent to enter that rest." Hebrews was written to believers—after the earthly ministry of Jesus. And it encourages them to "be diligent" to experience the rest that God has to offer. It's a warning to New Testament folks, saying, "Don't jump ship on sabbath rest!"

To borrow modern language, it's time to "lean in" on rest and examine it more fully.

For now, we are going to let this passage lead us back to the beginning of the biblical story to ask some important questions about rest:

- What is it about God's rest that sends us back to the beginning?

- What does it even mean when it says that God rested?

- How is God's rest defined?

As we've seen, Hebrews 4:8–11 links the two types of rest (God's rest and a believer's rest) together and suggests they are similar. If we can figure out how God rested, then we will be one step closer to finding out what kind of rest believers are called to today.

God Rested on the Seventh Day

By the seventh day God completed His work which He had done, and He rested on the seventh day from all His work which He had done. Then God blessed the seventh day and sanctified it, because in it He rested from all His work which God had created and made. (Genesis 2:2–3)

Our brief look at Hebrews 4 has brought us back to the beginning of the biblical story, the account of creation in Genesis 1:1–2:3. Specifically, what does it mean in Genesis 2:2–3 when it states that God rested on the seventh day? If we can determine what that means, we will be on our way to figuring out the nature of the rest that's available to believers.[11] Remember that Hebrews 4:10 tells us that these concepts (God's rest and a believer's rest) are similar in nature.

Let's look at what happened in the first chapter of Genesis, which will help us determine what it was that God stopped doing when He rested.

In the beginning God created the heavens and the earth. The earth was formless and void, and darkness was over the surface of the deep, and the Spirit of God was moving over the surface of the waters. (Genesis 1:1–2)

As we approach the story of creation, we know there are a number of ways it has been interpreted. But no matter what understanding one has of these events, I'm going to propose it can be generally understood as taking something from a chaotic and disordered state and getting it to a place where everything works. No matter what view one holds about its interpretation, the process of bringing order to the universe can be clearly seen in this creation account. Just look at how Genesis 1:2 describes the earth in the beginning. It's described as being "formless and void."

What does that even mean?

It almost seems like there was nothing there, but we know that wasn't the case because there was earth, and water seemed to be covering everything. Later in the story the waters will be separated and dry land will appear. So, the earth is there but it is described in the language of non-order and non-function. No plants growing, no animals, no people, no way to tell time, no mechanisms in place to regulate the seasons of life. Ultimately, this earth will house humanity, but it's nowhere close to ready in this beginning state.

A Place to Be . . .

The remainder of the chapter (Genesis 1:3–31) describes the process of how God gave order to the world. What does this order look like? Let's start by defining order as "giving everything a place to be" and see what this looks like in the opening chapter of the Bible.

God says, "Light . . . you go over there."

"Darkness . . . there."

"Water . . . here, land there."

"Sky . . . up there."

"Luminaries . . . you go up there in the sky."

I realize this is rather simplistic, but when God gave everything a place to be, He took control of the chaos and He brought order to it. This action says something about the very nature of God. He wants to fix the chaos in the world.

About every six months, I do this same thing to my garage. There's lots of stuff in my garage, and it's usually in some form of disordered chaos. When it gets really bad, I spend a day (or six) giving everything a place to be.

"Sharp tools with handles . . . you go over there."

"Old grubby shoes caked with mud . . . there."

"Fishing gear (that I haven't used in years) . . . here."

"Folding chairs . . . there."

"Hot-tub chemicals . . . way up there."

When I'm done with this process of ordering my garage, it usually looks pretty good. I'll grab my wife to show her how clean it is, but that's usually not enough. I'll post "before and after" pictures on social media and invite people over to see my work. I'm weird that way.

. . . and Something to Do

In God's story of creation, God gave everything a place to be (ordering the chaos), but He also gave everything a thing to do (a function).

"Land . . . you know where you are supposed to be, now I'm going to give you something to do. You grow stuff, and let animals walk around on you. That's your job."

"Waters . . . you are going to hold swarms of living creatures, and you'll be used to water the stuff growing on the land. That's your thing to do."

"Luminaries . . . you are going to rotate so that there are days, seasons, and years. Things will grow and life will flourish."

God is giving things a place to be and something to do. Then on day six, humans are created and they are given the same. What is it that humans are given to do? In Genesis 1:28, God says, "Be fruitful and multiply."

That is certainly something to do![12]

He also instructs humanity to "subdue" the earth and "rule" over the other living creatures. This is an important distinction given to humans in the creation account. God invites humanity to join Him as delegates in the process of ruling.

He invites humans to be on the earth ruling as His vicegerents.[13] These are humanity's place to be and thing to do!

Then on the seventh day (Genesis 2:1–3), God is done with His creative work, and He rests. Oftentimes this rest is portrayed as ceasing work and not doing anything for the purpose of recuperation. That's what many people think is going on here. But there is something perplexing about that premise. Let's ask the honest questions everyone is thinking:

> What's God doing resting and recuperating?
>
> Is God not all-powerful?
>
> Is He really tired?
>
> Does He really need a break?

I don't think there is much theological wiggle room to answer those last three questions with anything but "no, no, and no." An all-powerful God doesn't require rest to recuperate, so there must be something else happening in this passage. What are we missing? Why is it stated this way?

Extrabiblical Help

This is where we get some help from extrabiblical sources. Since the beginning of the twentieth century, archaeologists have unearthed thousands of tablets of ancient Near Eastern literature from Egyptian, Hittite, Mesopotamian, Babylonian, and other ancient cultures.[14] Stories found on some of these tablets explain the creation of the cosmos at the hands of pagan gods. In these stories the pagan gods often compete with each other for the right to set up and rule the cosmos.[15]

Interestingly, some of these pagan stories have similarities with the biblical creation story. This shouldn't be too surprising, since many of them were written in a similar time and ancient Near Eastern cultural tradition. Such stories were told in a format that the people of their context would understand. Some of these secular stories also include an element where the pagan deity rests at the end of the creation process.[16]

This is a similarity that suggests to us that we can possibly go to those stories to find a definition or an idea of how rest was viewed in that culture and in that time. If we can determine what rest means in those contexts, we may have some help in understanding what's going on in the biblical account.

In the extrabiblical accounts, the victorious pagan god usually builds a temple, moves into that temple, and takes command of the cosmos. In those accounts, this process of ruling the earth is described as "resting." This is the ancient idea of rest and several modern scholars have noticed this secular connection to the concept of biblical rest. One author in particular, Dr. John H. Walton, has written extensively on the topic. He has concluded that in the ancient Near Eastern world, rest was understood as what results when a crisis has been resolved or when stability has been achieved.

In those cultures, rest wasn't disengagement from the cares, worries, and tasks of life (on a beach vacation, lying in a hammock). Rather, rest is where the day-to-day routines are established. For ancient pagan gods, this meant they could oversee the day-to-day operations of the cosmos.

To bring this into more of a modern setting, Americans could use similar language for the person who rules from the White House. The president is elected and fills all the cabinet positions with the right people, and then moves into the White House and rules from the Oval Office.

Or consider the process that a new football coach goes through when hired by a university. The coach locates assistants to help organize and coordinate the team's defense, offense, and special teams. He recruits players to come to the school. He orders equipment and uniforms. Once all the pieces are in place and the season arrives, the coach can begin practices and prepare for the first game. In an ancient context, the end result in these two examples could be referred to as "resting."

Walton has said we should think of this idea of rest as "more a matter of engagement without obstacles . . . rather than disengagement without responsibilities."[17]

This is a key point for our entire study. The way we should understand rest at the end of the creation account in Genesis is more a matter of God's engagement without obstacles than His disengagement without responsibilities. When it says that God rested on day seven, He's not taking a day off. He's actually beginning His full engagement as ruler of the cosmos, now that His order has been established.

Adam and Eve at Rest with God

Why is all this important? Because Adam and Eve were originally at rest with God in the garden of Eden. Eden was the special place of God's presence, and like most temples in the ancient Near East it too was located on a mountain, with rivers of life flowing from it.[18] How do we know Adam and Eve were at rest? The text tells us this way:

> Then the LORD God took the man and put him into the garden
> of Eden to cultivate it and keep it. (Genesis 2:15)

God gave them a place to be and a thing to do! But several English translations veil the most important aspect of this verse. The word describing how God "placed" humanity in the garden is a Hebrew word for "rest."[19] It could be understood that God took the human and "rested him" in the garden to do his work. He was there to abide, rest, and take up residence.[20] The garden had been ordered and structured and humanity was at rest with God in that sacred space.[21] They were in their place, fulfilling their God-given role, and functioning the way they were intended to function.

Some like to think of Eden as the perfect world, but it wasn't. God created the function and order needed to assemble His entire kingdom, but He didn't originally create the completed product. Eden was really only the beginning of that process. God created all the parts and invited humanity to help Him with the assembly.

Lisa and I sometimes purchase furniture at IKEA. For those who don't know, IKEA is a company known for their wide variety of household furniture and goods. Their massive stores are organized as one never-ending maze of displays. They provide one section after another where they've staged their furniture to look like it can never look in *your* house. When we wander through their labyrinth, Lisa usually falls in love with something they've set out. She'll say something like, "Oh, wouldn't that look good in our bedroom?" And before I have time to respond, she's written down the number associated with the piece of furniture, and has already started skipping her way to the next adventure along their yellow-brick road.

That's usually when I start noticing a familiar pain on the top of my head. No, I haven't hit it on anything; I've just shopped here before. And I know the piece of furniture with which she fell in love is not the one they end up selling us. Their maze eventually leads to a gigantic warehouse where we find the number she wrote down and load a rectangular box into our cart.[22] The box contains all the pieces, but the furniture is not assembled. But not to worry—they provide a thirty-seven-page instruction manual which portrays a stick-figure person easily assembling the furniture. Even though I usually like the finished product, during the assembly process I've directed some very unholy comments toward that stick-figure character. I'm rarely able to fill his shoes!

In a similar way, God originally created a place for humanity, and provided all the pieces needed to assemble the finished product. But except for Eden, assembly wasn't included. And instead of providing a stick-figure instruction manual, the manufacturer followed humanity home to assemble the remaining creation as a joint venture. God knew if Adam and Eve fulfilled their fruitful mandate under His rule, Eden would need to expand into the unassembled parts of the world. In this way, His rule and order would spread to the entire creation.

The end of the biblical story describes a preview of this fully assembled kingdom. In Revelation 21–22, this new creation is described with several interesting features. We read about one of those features right away. The new creation doesn't have any sea (Revelation 21:1). This is sometimes understood as the lack of any large bodies of water, but, in the ancient Near Eastern culture, wild areas of the world were understood as *liminal space.*

"Liminal" is a term that describes an in-between state or transitional boundary between two places. I often think of the threshold of my front door as liminal space. When I'm in that place, I'm neither fully in my house, nor have I yet arrived outside. I'm in "liminal land."[23]

The ancient Near Eastern understanding of the world outside Eden would have included a liminal realm where God's rule was yet to be established or maintained. According to Walton, "The liminal realm existed on the periphery of creation and was home to dangerous animals; harsh and inedible plants; hostile terrain such as deserts, mountains, or the sea."[24]

So, in the biblical world of Genesis 2, the space outside the garden would have still included liminal land that would need to be subdued and brought under God's rule. But in Revelation 21, the absence of a sea is likely describing a world where all the liminal space within the creation has been brought under His authority. The end state describes a world where the rule of Eden has spread and consumed the entire creation. In the end, the assembly of the kingdom is complete. But that's at the end of the process.

According to Dr. Gregory Beale, "Because Adam and Eve were to subdue and rule 'over all the earth,' it is plausible to suggest that they were to extend the geographical boundaries of the garden until Eden covered the whole earth. They were on the primeval hillock of hospitable Eden, outside of which lay the inhospitable land. They were to extend the smaller liveable area of the garden by transforming the outer chaotic region into a habitable territory."[25]

When Adam and Eve are in the garden, we understand the world outside Eden as categorically different space. From their place in the garden, Adam and Eve began cultivating, keeping, subduing, and ruling within God's wisdom. They were operating in the seventh-day work of His rule. This is important because Adam and Eve's restful residence in Eden was conditional.

Do you know what happened next? Adam and Eve started working outside their God-given role. When they learned that the tree in the middle of the garden offered an opportunity to acquire "ordering wisdom," it sounded enticing. It was their chance to challenge the order that God had created and, like God, attempt to establish their own.

Their choice to eat from the tree was an effort to subvert His rule and gain the wisdom necessary to create their own system . . . to their own glory. It's first called the "tree of the knowledge of good and evil" (Genesis 2:17), but we later find out they understood it to be a source of ordering "wisdom" (Genesis 3:6). With that type of wisdom, they could create their own order and bring glory to themselves instead of God.

Their motives were symbolized by the shame of their nakedness. That's what they tried to cover, and that's why they hid from God. And since they thought they had a better plan, it's also the reason they were exiled. They stepped outside their "place" and "thing," and biblically speaking they were exiled from their rest and entered a place of unrest. Adam and Eve's rest was directly connected to the garden and submitting to God's rule. When they stopped observing God's rule, they stopped sharing in the rest that He offered.

In those early chapters of Genesis, Adam and Eve are presented as representatives for all of humanity. So, when they chose to leave *their* rest it also disrupted *humanity's* opportunity to live at rest. Do you remember the penalties Adam and Eve experienced? As a result of their choices, the land of their exile was cursed by God (Genesis 3:17). The land was removed from God's blessing, and any yield would now require painful labor.[26] Humanity's work in this curse-a-day land would be substantially different than the work they had experienced in the garden. Their things to do (be fruitful and multiply, subdue and rule) would now be done in a cursed land full of pain, toil, nuisance, and anxiety (Genesis 3:16–19).[27]

Eve would continue to follow God's mandate of fruitfulness, but now that process would be wrought with anxiety and trauma. Her trouble was not so much a description of the labor of giving birth, but the hardship of knowing the world into which her offspring would be born. Her anxious toil began with the news she had conceived. That's when she recognized her seed would come forth, grow, and someday face his own death. But she didn't yet understand the pain of also giving birth to the hand that would kill him.

Adam would follow God's mandate to cultivate and keep a garden, but now it would be outside Eden's rest. And like Eve, his work in a cursed land would also be filled with trauma. He would soon realize the struggle of creating order in his new existence. And he would now need to protect himself from others who would seek to establish their own. He would become weary from his lack of rest and recognize this as wages paid.

The exile of those representatives suggests that all of humanity will no longer instinctually desire to be where they were meant to be or do what they were meant to do in the way they were supposed to do it. Our whole existence will be restless.

If this is how we are to understand this idea of biblical rest, it is the same place humanity finds itself today. We are outside of Eden's rule. We try to do what we were made to do, but we are operating outside the function and order within which God created us to work. When this is how we function, we are in a state of unrest.

We are restless.

That's where the creation account leaves humanity. Then the biblical story continues with the descendants of Adam and Eve and the problems that ensued because of humanity's exile from rest.

But what would it mean for God to invite humanity back to a place of rest? It would be an invitation back to the function and order that God had originally planned. It would be an invitation to return to God's direction for us to use our talents to rule and subdue the earth.

Understanding humanity's unrest is just the first step in an IKEA-like labyrinth of interconnected ideas presented in the Bible. We're making good progress, but we've only just begun.

What Did God Do on the Eighth Day?

There's one additional aspect of the Genesis account of creation that further develops this understanding of God's seventh-day rest. In that first chapter of the Bible, the author uses a repetitive literary device to signify the end of each of the days of creation. It goes something like this: "There was evening and there was morning . . . an 'X' day." The author uses this phrase for each of the first six days of creation (Genesis 1:5, 8, 13, 19, 23, 31).

Authors generally use repetition like this for a reason. Repetition suggests congruity, builds familiarity, and establishes expectations for their readers. Repetition also develops a platform from which to jump when the author decides to break from its use.

In my early twenties, I taught junior high English and Language Arts in Puyallup, Washington. Those days were exhausting, but they were also some of the most fun I've had in my whole life. I used repetitive patterns each year to keep my students off-balance. One example of this happened as school began each fall. I would come the first day of school wearing a dress shirt and tie, giving homework to each class. They would receive the "shirt and tie/homework every night" routine for the first two weeks.

Then came Parent Night. It was an evening where the students stayed home and their parents came to campus and spent ten minutes in each of their children's classes with a five-minute passing time between presentations. It was a fast-paced schedule and many parents got lost wandering around the campus.

It was on Parent Night that I chose to break my repetitive pattern. On that night I wore a bathrobe (over my clothes) and slippers. Parents would come in, laugh a little at my costume, and listen to my description of their child's class. I would then dismiss them without much explanation of my attire.

The next day the students, having heard from their parents the night before, would come into class with questions about why I wore a bathrobe and slippers on Parent Night. But that next day I greeted the students in my regular shirt and tie, gave homework as usual, and suggested their parents might be a bit confused. I said it must have been one of their other teachers that did such an outlandish thing.

I played with them in this way for another week or so until I eventually wore the bathrobe and slippers during school. I established and broke from repetitive patterns like this the whole year. It kept my students off-balance and supplied me with the energy I needed to teach junior high![28]

Repetition can be used to establish a pattern, and also gather attention to highlight a change when that established pattern is abandoned.

Each of the first six days of creation end with the same repetitive phrase. "And there was evening and there was morning, the sixth day" (Genesis 1:31b). But on the seventh day of creation, the author abandons this literary device. After each of the first six days, the author has lulled us to sleep each day with his "evening and morning" formula. It's a pattern that signifies to readers the end of one particular activity and the beginning of another.

But this isn't the only example of literary repetition the author uses. At several points throughout the creation process God describes the different aspects of His creation as "good." In Genesis 1:4, God saw that the light was good. In Genesis 1:10, the separation of the dry land from the waters is also described as good. And so it is with each step of the creative process; with vegetation-bearing fruit and seeds (1:12), the lights governing the day and night (1:18), living creatures in the sea and in the air (1:21), and the beasts of the ground (1:25). In this context, "good" simply means that these items are in their "place to be" and are functioning properly.

But then on the sixth day that literary repetition is abandoned when the creation process is completed. "God saw all that He had made, and behold, it was very good" (Genesis 1:31a). This change, from "good" to "very good," signifies the end of something. For God, this is the end of His creative process. There will be no more giving function and order to the cosmos; that ordering work is complete. It is very good.

With the completion of that process the reader is poised to consider what's next. The seventh day and God's restful rule is what follows (Genesis 2:1–3). It is this seventh day that also lacks a mention of the evening/morning motif. The rapid changes from "good" to "very good" and the dropping of the evening/morning pattern signify a dramatic change in the story.

I often say that the seventh day of creation had no evening or morning. Of course, I mean this not literally, but literarily. What's the difference?

We know that the seventh day literally came to an end. How do we know this? Because we all went to bed last night and got up this morning. Today is a new day, and it's not the seventh day. But asking that same question from a literary perspective produces a dramatically different answer. Literarily speaking, the abandonment of the evening/morning repetition on the seventh day suggests that this day—or more accurately, the theological events of the day—never ended. This is a significant point in the narrative.

I usually highlight this by asking, "What did God do on the eighth day?" You may want to say that God returned to work on the eighth day. That would certainly line up with the example of the fourth commandment (six days on, one day off, then back to work again). Maybe you've always thought of God's rest, on the seventh day, as a one-day event in which God, even though He didn't need physical rest, modeled for humanity a physical day of rest which we are to imitate.

But surprisingly, the way the creation account is written suggests that the rest God entered into on the seventh day never ended. His rest continued on into the eighth day, the ninth, the tenth, and so on. This makes sense with the definition of rest we have identified thus far. On the sixth day God concluded His creative acts; everything had its place to be and thing to do. Then, on the seventh day, God began his rule over the cosmos, and that rule has never ended. It continues today. God continues to be fully engaged in the cosmos as its ruler. He is still "at rest."[29]

As Walton suggests, "God's rest did not involve relaxation but rule. Obviously we are not called to imitate his rule; we are called to acknowledge it and participate in it. On the sabbath we are to set aside our own attempts to bring order to our world by our own efforts."[30]

For a time, Adam and Eve did just that. They set aside any attempts to reorder the world and lived in relationship with God under his restful authority and reign. But when they stepped outside God's rule, and began to govern their own way of life, they were removed from the place of rest.

This situation created an important dilemma. God knows that, outside the garden, humans have poor memory. He knows that the further we get from Adam and Eve's experience of rest, the more humanity will forget that restful relationship ever existed. He knows we will begin to assume that what we are experiencing now, life outside the garden, is what God originally intended.

And He's right. Many have misunderstood the nature of the Eden experience and concluded that the way in which the world is functioning is just the way it is. One of my favorite sayings is, "It is what it is." But God is saying something different. He wants everyone to know, "This isn't what it was"—and maybe more importantly, "This isn't what it will be." God doesn't want His creation to forget this ancient truth.

So, God devised a plan to remind humanity that the world was once at rest, that rest is still available, and that it will one day be completely fulfilled.

CHAPTER 2

REMINDERS OF REST

Rest is a much bigger concept than we've considered thus far. As we have seen from Genesis 1–3, and the cultural context of similar creation accounts, God's rest should be understood much differently than time off of work. Rather, it's a description of the exercise of God's rule and authority over the creation to which He has given order and function. It's the idea that when everything is working the way it is supposed to, God is in control, everything is falling under His authority, and all creation is at rest.

This is how a believer's rest is qualitatively linked to God's rest. When people choose to fall under the authority of God's function and order of the cosmos, then they rest from their works as God did from His (Hebrews 4:10).

This Isn't the Way It's Supposed to Be

This chapter will likely challenge you with several paradigm shifts regarding the way you think about the story of the Old Testament. We are addressing the question of how God solved the problem of humanity living outside of God's rest.

It's a situation that was brought about by the decisions of humanity in the garden of Eden. It's a situation that God wanted desperately to solve. Now we begin to unpack God's plan to return humanity to a state of rest (living in close relationship with Him under His authority).

This dilemma reminds me of a scene from the 1991 movie *Grand Canyon*.[31] It's old enough now that I don't suspect many of you have seen it. It's a thoughtful movie featuring Danny Glover, Kevin Kline, Steve Martin, and Mary McDonald. One of the first scenes of the movie is sometimes referred to as the "tow-truck scene." Kevin Kline's character, an affluent businessman, is driving through a rough part of Los Angeles on his way home from a sporting event. It's a part of town that Kline's character would clearly not be comfortable walking through by himself.

As events in the scene play out, his car breaks down on the side of a fairly quiet street. These were the early days of car phones, and luckily his luxury car is equipped with this new technology, so Kline attempts to make a call for a tow truck. But his phone fails to connect so he finds a pay phone nearby. The tow company advises him to stay with his car until the truck arrives.

In the meantime, some young fellas from the area drive by and want to say hello. These young men are not as friendly as they could be. They are much more interested in harassing their out-of-place visitor than helping him find his way home. They stop and get out of their car, and the viewer gets the sense that something is about to go down. Kline could get his car stolen, or possibly something worse.

Just about that time, Danny Glover's character drives up in his tow truck. He pulls in front of the broken-down car and backs up to the front of it. Glover gets out, and without addressing the obvious situation playing out between Kline and his new friends, begins hooking his truck to the car.

Once the car is connected, Glover pulls the ringleader of the neighborhood gang aside and says to him, "I've got to ask you to let me go my way here." He explains that now that the man's car is connected to his truck, it's his responsibility.

Then Glover's character says something profound to the gang leader: "Man, the world ain't supposed to work like this. I mean, maybe you don't know that, but this ain't the way it's supposed to be. I'm supposed to be able to do my job without asking you if I can. That dude [Kline's character] is supposed to be able to wait with his car without you rippin' him off. Everything's supposed to be different than what it is."

Glover ends up talking his way out of the situation and he and Kline drive away. It's a profound scene. Glover's character comes in like a knight in shining armor (with crowbar in hand) and saves the day. It could be argued that he plays a type of Christ figure in the story as he saves Kline's character from a dilemma that Kline can't solve on his own.

But it's another aspect of that scene that reminds me of the situation we've been discussing thus far: it's the fact that humanity's no longer following God's original plan, but some of us don't know things are upside down.

So God, in a Danny Glover kind of way, decides to tell humanity, "This isn't the way it's supposed to be."

How does God choose to tell the world that things have gone awfully awry? He gives a restless humanity "reminders of rest." He gives the whole of creation reminders of the restful existence that humanity shared with God in the garden.

It's through the giving of these reminders that God says, "Maybe you don't know it, but this pain and toil you are experiencing isn't the way it's supposed to be. You were meant to be in your place and doing your thing without anything getting in the way of that. Everything is supposed to be different than what it is."

We see one of these reminders in Genesis 12:1–3, when God pulls a man named Abram out of the crowd of humanity and tells him to go forth "to the land which I will show you." God promises to show Abram his "place to be." It's a hyperlink[32] back to the story of Eden where God originally rested humanity in the garden.

God's promises include not just a land in which to live, but also numerous descendants that will become a large nation of people. It is through this nation that God will bless the whole earth. Then God gives Abram a new name, Abraham, which suggests he will be the father of a multitude (Genesis 17:5). That's certainly something to do! Abraham now has "a place to be" and a "thing to do," and he obeys God.

Abraham sets out, following God's direction, in search of the land that God had promised. The New Testament informs us that when Abraham set out, he was "looking for the city which has foundations, whose architect and builder is God" (Hebrews 11:10). We know that when the descendants of Abraham eventually take possession of the land under Joshua's leadership, that land is directly associated with God's rest (Joshua 1:10–18; 21:43–44; 23:1–3). But that doesn't mean people were just constantly lying around in hammocks!

It was a land where the rule and authority of God was to reign supreme. It was a land where the people were supposed to be functioning the way humanity was originally intended to function—a people who were trusting God, falling under His authority, and being blessed through this type of relationship. Ultimately, it was supposed to be a reminder of the garden of Eden experience humanity had before they were exiled into unrest.

God intended Abraham's descendants to be this little oasis in a world of dysfunction. This group of people living on a piece of land under the authority of God was to be a witness to the rest of the world. It should have reminded humanity that really, "*this* is the way it's supposed to be."

As the story continues, Abraham dies without personally experiencing all the promises of which God had spoken. But that's OK, because most of the promises were intended to be realized by his offspring. Unfortunately, Abraham's descendants don't end up in the Promised Land, but in Egypt . . . as slaves.

Let's consider this situation theologically for a moment. Slavery is the most dysfunctional type of work for humanity. Back in Eden, God had given people a restful place to be and a thing to do, and they followed His direction (at least for a while). The fall from that rest was when humanity received direction from someone other than God and then decided to follow that master instead.

What is slavery? Slavery is when someone takes the place of God and decides what *another* human is going to do for work. This is the most dysfunctional picture of the cosmos that can be painted, and unfortunately it is where unrest naturally leads. It is out of that dysfunction that God rescues Abraham's descendants, and He begins inserting reminders of rest for these people as He leads them to a land of rest.

Reminders of Rest

Now we begin to look more closely at the reminders of rest that God gave to those He saved from slavery in Egypt. Remember, God is giving His creation reminders that this isn't the way it's supposed to be, and in this part of the story He's working through a specific group of people. God reveals Himself to Moses through a complex set of instructions about how to live under His rule and authority. When these instructions are written down and presented to the people, they become the Law of Moses. It's a law that is often studied and dissected into smaller categories, but let's consider each of the individual parts of the Mosaic Law as small pieces of the whole. It's along this continuum, the whole Law, that God presents an ever-expanding portrayal of what rest originally was.

The group coming out of Egypt were some of the physical descendants whom God had promised to Abraham back in Genesis 12. God's promise also included a place to be (the Promised Land) and a thing to do (live at rest with God and thus bless the whole world through their example). Abraham didn't receive all of this, and his immediate children didn't either. And at this point in the story, four hundred years had passed without God's promise progressing as Jacob's descendants expected. But now, in the book of Exodus, this particular generation is brought out of slavery and the storyline progresses fairly rapidly.

Manna in the Wilderness

Exodus opens with Moses negotiating the release of the Israelites from slavery. It's an epic tale, to be sure (Exodus 1–14). Pharaoh, the Egyptian ruler, was unwilling to release the Israelites from their bondage. But then God sends Moses in to broker the release agreement and, after a series of ten plagues, Pharaoh agrees to let the Israelites leave with Moses. As they leave the land, Pharaoh reneges on the agreement and, with his army, pursues his former slaves. Pharaoh's army is eventually consumed by the waters of the Red Sea.[33] The Israelites, under Moses's leadership and by the hand of God, have been released from slavery. They find themselves in the desert lacking water and food, items that had been plentiful in Egypt.

It's into this setting that God begins to remind them of a time, well before the Egyptian slavery, when God supplied humanity with bountiful amounts of food and water in the garden of Eden. The first of these reminders shows up in Exodus 16 when God gave them manna in the wilderness. We could get lost in a conversation about what this manna was. We're not sure. They weren't sure either—the Hebrew word *manna* literally means "What is it?" (Exodus 16:15). But let's not get so focused on the logistics of the manna that we miss the theology of this gift.

God brings this group of people to a place where he provides food for them on a daily basis. All they have to do is get up in the morning and harvest the food that's been provided. Does this type of situation sound familiar at all?

It should!

That was the situation in the garden of Eden. In the beginning, God had planted the vineyards and caused everything to grow (Genesis 1:11; 2:8–9) and told humanity to eat what He had supplied (Genesis 1:29; 2:15–16). This group of Abraham's descendants hadn't experienced anything like that in Egypt. So when they escape the slavery of Pharaoh, God first gives them the manna. It's a reminder that it didn't use to be the way it is. It used to be that God provided food and that humanity's job was to get up in the morning, trust God, and eat.

In this same episode God gives them another reminder. He instructs the people to collect a double portion of manna on the sixth day, and to not work on the seventh. What's happening here? Well, it's another reminder of proper functioning. God asks the people to enter into a trust relationship with Him. He is saying: do this, but don't do that. Does that sound familiar at all?

God had set up a similar trust relationship with Adam and Eve in Eden before the fall (Genesis 2:16–17). This type of trust relationship says, "I know it's your job to give me a place to be and directions regarding how to do what I was created to do, and I'll follow your directions."

How did this end up for the recently emancipated Israelites? Well, they started out grumbling and complaining (Exodus 16:2), and along the way they didn't follow instructions very well (Exodus 16:27–28).

What is grumbling and complaining? Ultimately it is a lack of trust in God's ability to provide the way it was originally intended to be provided. So, given the lack of food, they grumbled and complained. They're coming out of four hundred years in Egypt, so let's give them a little break regarding their response. But let's not miss what God is doing. He is giving the people reminders. Think of these as small steps that encourage the people to reestablish a right relationship with their Creator. They are traveling on a road to rest. God wants them to start heading down Sabbath Street.

Was the people's unfaithful response a surprise to God? Did their lack of trust cause Him to abandon the plan to provide more reminders of rest?

No, because the plan to give these reminders was always bigger than just the manna.

The Fourth Commandment

The next reminder of rest in the text is found in Exodus 20:8–11, the fourth commandment. Listen to the language of this statement:

Remember the sabbath day, to keep it holy. (v. 8)

In context, that's obviously a commandment to remember the repetitive seventh day of every week that God is asking the people to observe. But when the people remember the seventh day of every week, what are they also supposed to remember? They are to remember that on the original seventh day, God rested. It's a hyperlink back to that original rest. That first day of rest is the "sabbath" the people are really supposed to recall.

So now God is asking the people to trust Him every day with the manna, and also on the seventh day to do no work. But let's examine this a little more. Does that mean they can't do anything? I'm going to suggest that in this commandment, God is giving instruction to cease only our dysfunctional work, the type of work we accomplish under the curse. You remember the curse that was handed down to humanity at the fall from rest (Genesis 3:17–19). We will take a closer look at this concept from a New Testament perspective in chapter 4.

For now, let's just ask this question: When God says, "Don't do work," do you think God is saying, "Don't use the gifts I've given you to do the things I've given you to do under my rule and authority as Creator of the cosmos"?

Not at all!

In fact, that's one of the points Jesus makes with the Pharisees in the New Testament. He says it's OK to do "good" on the sabbath (Matthew 12:12). What's doing good? It's being in your place and doing what you are supposed to be doing under God's rule. You are always supposed to be doing that type of work.

That's what sabbath is.

That's what rest is.

When God restricts work in the fourth commandment, His instructions don't apply to all types of work. He's only restricting us from the pain and toil type work we experience in the curse-a-day world.[34] He's saying, "One day a week, stop going outside my prescribed place to be and thing to do. Stop choosing what Adam and Eve chose."

Let's ask another question. When the commandment says "to keep it holy" (Exodus 20:8), what's the best way to keep a day holy? It's to be in your God-given place and to do your God-given thing under God's rule.

To be obedient and to trust—that's what's supposed to be happening on the seventh day.

So how did it go with the people in the wilderness? Well, we find out a little later in the story. There is a man who goes out on the sabbath day and gathers wood (Numbers 15:32–36). What's the end result? Those who caught the man didn't know what to do with him, so they took him to Moses. But Moses didn't know what to do either, so he asked God— and God gave instructions to kill the man!

This is where we could get stuck in our conversation about this event. We surmise, "Wasn't that kind of harsh punishment for a guy picking up sticks?"

We might think, "This doesn't seem at all like the God of the New Testament."

In some ways I might agree with you, but let's not get distracted by that cul-de-sac conversation in which we usually get stuck. Let's step back and look at the theology that this story presents.

Let me restate it this way: a man, who's supposed to be resting (and we now know what rest is), decides to not follow God's commandment but instead goes out and does what he wants to do and the penalty is death. Does that sound familiar at all?

It should!

That's exactly what happened in the garden of Eden. It was there that humanity was given a place to be and a thing to do. Then they decided to step outside that thing to do, and what was the penalty?

Death.

This guy in Numbers 15 becomes a very vivid reminder that, "This isn't the way it's supposed to be." Let's also point out that not everyone who broke the sabbath was put to death, but this man was the first breaker of the covenant, and God dealt pretty harshly with him to make a point.[35] Does it mean he didn't get to be in heaven, just because he broke the sabbath? Well, I expect to see a lot of Old Testament characters in heaven who did a lot worse. I believe we can comfortably leave that decision to God's justice, mercy, and grace.

With all that said, let's ask the question a second time: Even though following the sabbath didn't go very well, did God abandon the idea of giving ever-increasing reminders of how it was in days gone by? No. He didn't stop because He knew that this picture was bigger than just the manna, and was even bigger than the fourth commandment.

Festivals and Additional Sabbath Days

Together with the daily giving of manna and the weekly sabbath, God gave the people seven festivals to be celebrated each year during the agricultural harvest seasons. These festivals added additional sabbath days, linked not directly to the seventh-day rest cycle but to the yearly calendar (Leviticus 23:3, 7–8, 21, 24–32, 35–39). So now, in addition to the weekly reminders, the people have a yearly rhythm of remembering that trusting God's rule leads to an uncommon type of rest.

Those in the Christian tradition may be familiar with some of these festivals. Three of them—Passover, Unleavened Bread, and First Fruits[36]—were to be celebrated at the time of the barley harvest in the spring. Then fifty days later, at the time of the wheat harvest, they were to celebrate the Feast of Weeks (or Pentecost). In the fall (at the time of the fruit and nut harvests) they celebrated the Feast of Trumpets, the Day of Atonement, and the Feast of Booths (or tabernacles).[37]

As we add these reminders to our list, I'd like you to begin seeing these items as strategically interconnected and positioned like an inverted funnel that starts small with the manna, then expands a little with the weekly sabbath, and now is getting bigger by adding several other sabbath days to the yearly calendar.

God knew that the repetition of manna every day, and the weekly sabbath schedule, might get mind-numbingly mundane. That's often what happens with repetitive events; over time they lose their effectiveness. So God added additional days, attached to a program of yearly festivals. In this way it was to become an ever-expanding picture of people living under God's rule in a relationship of rest.

Sabbatical Year

The coordinated, funnel-like, ever-expanding system of "rest reminders" grew even bigger with the addition of the sabbatical year. We are introduced to the sabbatical year as a sabbath rest for the land.

> You shall sow your land for six years and gather in its yield, but on the seventh year you shall let it rest and lie fallow, so that the needy of your people may eat: and whatever they leave the beast of the field may eat. You are to do the same with your vineyard and your olive grove. (Exodus 23:10–11)

Does this description remind you of anything? (I hope you saw this one on your own before I asked the question.) It's a hyperlink back to the original purpose given to the land at creation.

What does it even mean for the land to be at rest? It's not a living entity, is it? I'm not sure if you've noticed, but it's difficult to get dirt to relax in a hammock! That's not what it's talking about at all.

Let's remember what rest is. Rest is being in your place and doing the thing that God intended you to do. For land, what was its original intended purpose? It was supposed to grow stuff (Genesis 1:10–12), let living creatures crawl around on it (Genesis 1:24–25), and let those creatures eat the stuff that grows (Genesis 1:29–30). Land, that's your job.

How did this change after the fall from rest? The picture is that there is something substantial that changed the way the land worked. After the fall, man had to work the land instead of just naturally allowing things to grow. It was under man's efforts and toil (pain) that the land would produce food.

Lisa and I currently live in a very agricultural part of Oregon, the Willamette (wuh-la-muht) Valley. In fact, the property right across the street from our house is farmland. There are acres and acres of land that someone else takes care of, and it's all for our viewing pleasure! Every year we get to see the land tilled, then planted, then sprayed and fertilized. We watch the plants grow, become mature, and then eventually be harvested. Then the whole process starts over. It is quite a coordinated effort to make all that happen.

Sometimes the farmer who oversees the land across the street will let the land just sit for a growing season. He won't plant anything, and do you know what usually happens? There are some seeds left over from the last harvest that take root and just naturally grow. It's random, and there is not nearly as much as when it's a planned effort, but some plants just naturally grow.

What is the sabbatical year? It's a picture of letting the land function the way it was originally intended to function. Notice the instructions: don't go out and plant your crops, just let them grow naturally, the way they were originally intended to grow. Also notice who is supposed to receive the yield. Is it each farmer that receives his own crop? No. Everyone gets to eat. The needy people (Exodus 23:11) have as much right to the produce of the land as anyone else.

Let me ask this question: In the sabbatical year, are there any needy people? Well, if their need is food, there's not. Everyone is on an equal playing field in the sabbatical year. Even the beasts of the field are included, just as it was in the beginning. This is how it was originally when everything was at rest.

This is an important step in God's progression. He is building in reminders of the way it was supposed to be so people will remember that rest not only was, but still is, the gold standard.

Was this the end of reminders of rest? Nope. God's plan was bigger than the manna, the fourth commandment, the additional sabbath days attached to the festivals, and even the sabbatical year. What could be bigger than that? Well just read on . . . because it's "inconceivable"!

The Year of Jubilee

The term "jubilee" refers to a time of celebration and emancipation. Just as the seventh-day sabbath expanded to the sabbatical year, the sabbatical year idea culminates in the Year of Jubilee (Leviticus 25:8–22). This was to happen every fiftieth year. The idea is to count seven sets of seven years. In the forty-ninth year, what's happening? Well, that's a sabbatical year and no one is planting crops. Then the fiftieth year is the Year of Jubilee. What happens then?

It's a crazy year. Why would I call it crazy? Because nobody on Earth would ever naturally choose to live this way. Why? Because of the fall from rest. That's the only reason.

God gives the descendants of Abraham this Year of Jubilee as a dramatic picture and reminder of what once was. God says, everything you did in the previous sabbatical year, I want you to do that again. You are going to allow the land to grow produce again the way it was originally intended.

God then instructs them to do something else that will seem absurd. In the last fifty years it's likely that someone has gotten themselves in a bit of financial trouble and had to sell their land and move. That happens all the time in a fallen world. In this fiftieth year we are going to reset everything. That means we are going to give land back to its original owners. By doing this, everyone will go back to the way it was in the beginning.

God says there are some who, in the last fifty years, have gotten into even more financial trouble and selling their land didn't completely solve the problem. They've actually had to take on debt and become slaves. This is the most dysfunctional picture of rest there is. So what are we going to do in this Year of Jubilee?

We're going to hit the reset button. We're forgiving debt, which will allow people to break free from financial slavery. And they will have the freedom to go back to the place they were originally given to live (their place to be). With these provisions, what do people now have the freedom to do? They can live at rest under God's rule, in a land of rest.[38]

That's a crazy year for sure, but don't get caught up in the discussion of how nutty this idea is or how practically impossible it would be to pull something like this off, and miss the theology behind it. It's a picture of a reset to a time with no earthly masters telling slaves what to do. It's a picture of God and humanity working together within the relationship they were meant to have. Every fifty years everyone has the freedom to go back to their place, and ask the question, "What's my thing to do?"

The Sign of the Covenant

All these reminders of rest were part of a much larger covenant God made with the nation of Israel. Covenants are agreements between parties. They hold some of the same qualities of our modern contracts, but a covenant is more than that. It's a spiritual pledge.

We still have some examples of covenants in our modern culture. For some, the institution of marriage is one such illustration. Lisa and I were married in December of 1990. On that dark and stormy night,[39] we entered into a covenantal relationship with each other. If you had been at the ceremony, you would have heard us exchange vows of a spiritual nature. Then we exchanged rings. We both agreed that those rings would be a "sign," or reminder, of the promises we made to each other that day. We've worn our reminders of that covenant almost every day since (there was that time when I accidentally lost my ring in our kitchen garbage for a couple of days).

Covenants in the Bible also have "signs," or reminders, to the parties involved that a covenant is in place. Those familiar with the biblical story are probably already aware of some of these. For instance, when the Lord made a covenant with humanity through Noah (Genesis 9:11–17), He gave the "sign" of the rainbow as a confirmation and reminder of that covenant. When God established a covenant with Abraham (Genesis 17:9–14), He established the "sign" of circumcision.

According to Walton and Longman, "These signs are like brands. They serve as a reminder to the covenant partners of the relationship established between them. . . . Signs are, not surprisingly, integrally related to the specific character of the covenant they are attached to."[40]

It might be surprising to learn, then, that for the covenant God established with the people at Mt. Sinai, the "sign" of that covenant was God's sabbaths.

The LORD spoke to Moses, saying, "But as for you, speak to the sons of Israel, saying, 'You shall surely observe My sabbaths; for this is a sign between Me and you throughout your generations, that you may know that I am the Lord who sanctifies you. Therefore you are to observe the sabbath, for it is holy to you.'" (Exodus 31:12–14a)

Let's notice a couple things about this short passage. First, the sabbaths God handed down through Moses are described as *God's* sabbaths; He calls them "My sabbaths." The people were not told to observe *their* sabbaths; they are of the Lord's design. When humanity is brought back to a proper understanding of rest, it is the Lord's rest to which we are invited. It is not our idea of rest. For so many today, the understanding of sabbath is that it is their possession; that they get to decide what it is and how to do it. But humanity doesn't control sabbath rest. Sabbath rest is God's creation, and in the New Testament Jesus claims lordship of that reality (Matthew 12:8; Mark 2:28; Luke 6:5).

The next point is a grammatical distinction between the plural and singular use of the word. In verse 13, God instructs that the people are to observe "My sabbaths" (plural). Then in verse 14, He says they are to observe "the sabbath" (singular), referring specifically to the weekly sabbath. Some assume that both of these references refer to the same thing. They conclude that "My sabbaths" (plural) must be the collection of all the weekly sabbath (singular) days. But that's not what the grammar suggests, and it's not what God is communicating.

We've just unpacked the full theology of sabbath rest presented in the Mosaic Law. We now know that the weekly sabbaths are just a small portion of a larger sabbath system. The sign of the Mosaic covenant is not just the weekly sabbath days; rather, the "sign" is the whole theology of the ever-expanding picture of sabbath rest we've discussed. When the Israelites observed the weekly sabbaths, festival sabbaths, sabbatical years, and years of jubilee, they were participating in "*the* sign of their covenant."

God's instruction then, in verse 13, is to observe "My sabbaths"—that is, the long list of those reminders of rest He had just handed down to Moses. Then, in verses 14–17, he gives the example of just one of those reminders: the weekly sabbath. When the people observed all the sabbaths described in the Mosaic Law, they were signaling, to God, themselves, and the rest of the world that they were parties to the covenant.

The problem is, the descendants of Abraham never fully did this. They never fully adopted the sign of the covenant which God had given them. They failed to correctly observe "God's sabbaths" in the way He had described. And years later in their story, the prophet Ezekiel would describe God's response to their lack of obedience:

> So, I took them out of the land of Egypt and brought them into the wilderness. I gave them My statutes and informed them of My ordinances, by which, if a man observes them, he will live. Also, I gave them My sabbaths to be a sign between Me and them that they might know that I am the Lord who sanctifies them. But the house of Israel rebelled against Me in the wilderness. They did not walk in My statutes and they rejected My ordinances ... and My sabbaths they greatly profaned. (Ezekiel 20:10–13)

That was true of the first generation in the wilderness, but it was also true of the people after they entered the Promised Land. Israel's practice of the sabbaths was corrupted by their own ideas of what it should be. They changed the sign of the covenant and adapted it for their own purposes. They added their own meanings and chose to never include key parts of the covenantal sign. For instance, Israel never observed the Year of Jubilee the way it was described to them. That once-a-generation celebration was to be the most profound picture to humanity of what it is like to live at rest with God, but that illustration of rest was never completed.

Consider those who paint pictures on canvas. If someone paints a picture and doesn't finish it, or if they only put in certain parts of the picture but leave other sections unfinished, those viewing the piece of art never get to see everything they are supposed to see. They don't ever see the beauty that only the finished painting can portray.

A quick search on the internet will bring up many examples of unfinished paintings. Sometimes artists get distracted, sometimes they die before they can finish the work, but sometimes the subjects don't come back for a second sitting. That was the case for artist Alice Neel in 1965. She started a portrait of James Hunter, a draftee who was about to go to Vietnam. In the first sitting the artist was able to complete the pensive head of James Hunter, resting on one hand while he sat in a chair. She had just enough time in that first sitting to draw a rough outline of the remainder of Hunter's body and the chair in which he was sitting. The draftee was supposed to come back for a second sitting to allow Neel to finish her work, but he never came back. To this day there is a bit of a mystery as to why he was a no-show for his second sitting. No one knows if he had a change of heart or if something more serious might have happened to him.[41]

But what was the result of his no-show? The painting became famous and remains unfinished to this day. Some details, one of his hands and his head, are clearly portrayed, and the rest of the picture is only in outline form. Interestingly, even though it's obvious the picture was never completed, the unfinished work is now considered to be a finished product.

That's similar to the theological picture of rest. These reminders of rest, culminating in the Year of Jubilee, were intended to be a picture of another time and another place, but the last part of the painting was never fully finished. There's a rough outline of it in the biblical text, but the Year of Jubilee and other parts of the picture never made it back for the second sitting.

The Land as Rest

In the beginning of the book of Joshua, the people remember the words of Moses: "The LORD your God gives you rest [*a place to be and a thing to do under his rule*] and will give you this land" (Joshua 1:13).

What's going on here?

These reminders of rest don't just apply then to days and years and the release of debt, but to the actual physical land itself. God intended for this land of Israel, and the people living within its boundaries under His rule and authority, to be a picture for the whole world. It was to be a picture that things had functioned differently in the past, and that one day they would return to the way it was supposed to be. It was to be a message that God's purpose is to bring order and function back to the chaos of a fallen world. That's His purpose. While that ultimate plan is playing out, He is giving reminders to creation so they won't forget where they are in the picture.

It was before and it will be again; just remember this isn't the way it's supposed to be. As you probably know, it didn't go very well when the descendants got into the land. They distorted the reminders of rest so much that it distracted the people from remembering the very thing God wanted them to understand.

I think in many ways this is similar to where the church finds itself today in its conversation about rest. Rest has become so distorted and applied out of context that believers are distracted from remembering what it is that they are supposed to remember: God has a plan for a complete reset.

And thank God He does!

Looking for a City

Now back to Hebrews, the New Testament book that pulls Old Testament references together to weave the biblical narrative into a New Testament context. It says in chapter 11, verses 8–16, "By faith Abraham, when he was called, obeyed by going out to a place which he was to receive as an inheritance; and he went out, not knowing where he was going."

Do you see the way this is worded? God told Abraham he had a place to be, so by faith Abraham left his old place in search of the new place. He didn't know where the land was, or even exactly what he was supposed to do once he arrived. Abraham knew he wasn't where he was supposed to be, and so he became more interested in finding his place than protecting his possessions. This is a great picture of trusting in God's rule!

As the account goes, Abraham doesn't receive the land he was promised. His wife Sarah, walking alongside in faith, doesn't receive it. His son Isaac and his grandson Jacob (heirs to the same promise) don't receive it either (Hebrews 11:9–11). God's promise was much bigger than any one of these individual people. The text says that all these people died without actually receiving these things, but understood they would be coming. They confessed that they were "strangers and exiles on the earth."

We often read this statement as suggesting, "They lived as strangers here on the earth because they really should have been living with God in the heavens."[42] But that's not what it's saying. It's saying that they were strangers here on the earth because they realized something else: this isn't the way the earth is supposed to be.

That's what made them strangers here on the earth, because the rule of earth is supposed to be different. That's what makes believers today aliens as well. Let me paraphrase Hebrews 11:13 for perspective: "All these died in faith, without receiving that oasis that was promised to them. But having envisioned that oasis of rest and having welcomed it from a distance they said, 'We don't belong here. We don't belong to the administration that currently rules this fallen world. We recognize and give witness to a different way this whole thing was supposed to be.'"

Then the writer of Hebrews says something incredibly profound in 11:14: "For those who say such things make it clear that they are seeking a country of their own." They were promised a place—and they are seeking a "fatherland" (in the original language) of their own.

Indeed, if they had been thinking of that country from which they went out, they would have had opportunity to return. But as it is, they desire a better country, that is, a heavenly one. (Hebrews 11:15–16)

These people of faith desired a different administration than the one under which the world currently operates. But when it says they were seeking a "heavenly one" don't get lost in what you think that means. It doesn't mean they were wanting to die and go to heaven. Rather, it is describing their desire to remain on this earth and live here under a new administration, because the current way it is operating isn't right. They are seeking the administration that ruled in the beginning, the one that will one day rule again completely unhindered.

They are saying, "I desire the restful rule established long ago in Eden."

When Abraham is given the promise, that's what he's seeking. Go back and read the Genesis 3:21–24 account of the exile from the garden. When Adam and Eve are kicked out, the garden of Eden doesn't disappear. It remains right where it was, with the cherubim and a flaming sword in place to guard the entrance. At least theologically, Eden still exists. It is the place of God's rule on earth. It's the continuation of His rest.

When Abraham is given a better promise, he goes out in search of a better country. It's a heavenly country where God's rule and administration reigns, and it's on the earth. Abraham is looking for the rest originally offered in Eden.

"Therefore, God is not ashamed to be called their God; for He has prepared a city for them" (Hebrews 11:16). What is this passage saying? The reader gets to see this city at the very end of the book of Revelation. In Revelation 21, the new creation is described as a city and the building blocks are people. The city is its people, and their final destination is not to stay in heaven—it's to return God's rule and authority back to the earth. The whole goal is to restore a fully realized creation that began on the seventh day: a creation at rest.

The author of Hebrews wants us to remember the city where God's rule offers everyone a place to be and an unhindered thing to do. Despite the dysfunction, pain, and toil in the world, that city still exists.

Let's not forget to ask the question, "What's available to believers today?" What part of this idea of rest is available now? Do you remember the message we've discussed in Hebrews 4?

So there remains a Sabbath rest for the people of God. For the one who has entered His rest has himself also rested from his works, as God did from His. Therefore, let us be diligent to enter that rest. (Hebrews 4:9–11)

Those who come to faith enter into a rest similar to the rest that God is experiencing. So, what is the author of Hebrews talking about? That's exactly what we'll explore as we progress deeper into this study.

ADDITIONAL REST RESOURCES

CHAPTER 3

IMAGE-BEARING AND SHADOW-CASTING

You have formed us for Yourself, and our hearts are restless till they find rest in You.

—Augustine of Hippo[43]

In the previous chapters we have used some common language to describe rest, but we've moved past the modern cultural understanding of those terms. We've become acquainted with the biblical definitions for that vocabulary. So how are we rethinking this ancient concept? Let's do a little review, and then continue to build on those ideas.

We've seen how God's rest is first pictured in Genesis where it's presented as God's rule over an ordered creation. It's God's never-ending, active engagement over the cosmos as its King. It's a story where He gave everything a place to be, a thing to do, and in the beginning humanity's representatives were at rest with Him in the garden. Adam and Eve were in their place and doing their thing, at rest, as long as they acknowledged God as their ruler. Now, let's look a little more closely at some of the characteristics of that restful relationship Adam and Eve had before the fall.

Bearing God's Image[44]

> God created man in His own image, in the image of God He created him; male and female He created them. (Genesis 1:27)

Humanity was the only part of creation that was given the unique distinction of being made in God's image. So, what exactly does that mean? To be sure image-bearing is a multifaceted concept that I won't try to fully address here. Rather, let me present one important aspect of this concept we notice directly from the text.

Biblically speaking, the word used for "image" is sometimes also translated as "idol." That's how the word is most often used in the rest of the Old Testament. For instance, this same Hebrew word describes statues (images) of pagan gods (Numbers 33:52; 2 Kings 11:18; 2 Chronicles 23:17; Ezra 7:20; Ezekiel 16:17; Amos 5:26). The biblical understanding of an idol (image) is something that represents the likeness of something else, the thing it represents. This is sometimes a physical similarity that the idol depicts, but it can be much more than that too.

For example, sometimes children bear a physical likeness to their parents. Is that true in your family? In my case, I am much more like my dad in physical stature, and my sister Jodi was more like my mom. My dad, Larry, was six feet, four inches tall and was a football lineman in high school (back when they played with leather helmets and no face guards). Dad was a big dude.

On the other hand my mom, Eleanor, is five feet, four inches tall, and she fits nicely under my armpit if I lift one hand up and over her head. I do a good job of bearing my father's physical image, but that's not the end of the comparisons.

When my dad was young, he lived in Seattle, Washington. We have extended family in that area and I grew up visiting there at least once a year for Hall-family gatherings. At a certain point during every trip, as our immediate family drove through the middle of Seattle on Interstate 5, my dad would stop whatever conversation was happening in the car and announce, "We are now crossing over the location of my childhood home." It was the one he lived in as a young adolescent through the time he was in high school. As it turns out, the city purchased, and eventually demolished, his parents' house because it was right in the middle of one of the northbound lanes (or at least it eventually would have been).

This type of behavior was one of my dad's consistent character traits. Any time we passed by a place with any amount of personal historical significance, he would stop the conversation, point the place out, and recount his connection. He would often drive miles out of the way to visit such places. This happened quite often and I remember thinking, in my arrogant adolescence, that this character trait was ridiculous.

Then it happened.

I grew up and had a family of my own, and now I do the very same thing! When Lisa and I drive anywhere close to one of our former homes, I instinctively feel the urge to meander my way through the familiar streets and end up driving slowly by our old domicile. One or two turns into the journey, when Lisa realizes what I'm doing, she usually comments, "Oh, you're just like your dad!"

And that's a good thing.

I bear my dad's image in many different ways: the way I look, the way I talk, the way I burp, and yes, even the way I drive slowly by former places of residence to make reminiscent comments.

In Genesis 1:27 the "image-bearing" characteristic that God shared with humanity could refer to just a physical likeness, or it might describe some of humanity's metaphysical characteristics, like having a conscience and the ability to reason. To be sure, both of these options are worthy of further comment in the discussion of things we share with the Creator. But there is a different aspect of this image-bearing that we find in the Genesis text. In Genesis 1:27, the "made in God's image" statement is followed directly with a job description:

God created man in His own image, in the image of God He created him; male and female He created them. God blessed them
and said to them, "Be fruitful and multiply, and fill the earth and
subdue it; and rule over the fish of the sea and over the birds
of the sky and over every living thing that moves on the earth."
(Genesis 1:27–28)

This passage suggests that a large part of our image-bearing is
reflected in what we do and how we do it. In this context image-bearing is presented in terms of a "functional reflection" of the image. In
other words, when we are in our God-given place to be and we are
doing our God-given thing to do (the way God would have us do it),
we are functionally bearing God's image to the world. We are acting
just like God would if He were here in the flesh. Does that sound
familiar to you?

It might, because it's very similar to what Jesus asks of New Testament believers. We are to have a heart after God that should play out very
practically in the way we live our lives. We are to love others the way God
loves us (1 John 4:11–19), be willing to forgive often as God does (Matthew 18:21–22), and trust the circumstances of our lives to the one who
is really in control of such things (Matthew 6:25–34).

In this way we are to bear His image within creation. God is sharing His responsibilities with humanity; subduing, ruling, cultivating, and
keeping are all God activities. Those are things God does, but at creation
He agreed to share those activities with humanity. We have all been called
to reflect God's image by being in our right place, at the right time, and
respond the way God would have us respond. That's a huge privilege and
it's an even bigger responsibility.

The image of God that humanity shares is an invitation to be and act
like God on earth. When we do the things God would do, in the place
that He would have us do them, we are bearing His image and reflect-
ing His rest. This revelation isn't anything new. It is just a little twist on

the popular 1990s question asked on thousands of bumper stickers and bracelets, "What would Jesus do?" (WWJD). Except this time, we are asking, "What's my place to be and thing to do?" (WMPTBATTD). That acronym just doesn't roll off the tongue quite as well.

Are We Just Bystanders?

I like to create sprinkler systems. It's one of the things I do. I'm even pretty good at it. I've installed in-ground sprinklers for the last three homes we've owned. In this process I do the initial layout of the system on paper, get some help creating a parts list, purchase all the equipment, dig the trenches, piece everything together, make sure all the pipes are glued, bury them, and plant the grass. It's quite a process and I'm usually ready to be done with it by the end of each project.

Now I want you to imagine something. Let's say you walk by my house when I'm beginning to dig the trenches for a new sprinkler system. Perhaps you would stop and comment on what a masterful job I was doing. Maybe you would even ask a couple of questions about how the system will operate when I'm done, what type of sprinklers I'm using, or if it also has a drip system attached.

Let's say you ask all these questions, listened to my answers, and then remained in my driveway for the rest of the day offering me further compliments regarding how good everything looks. Do you know what I would do? I'd invite you to join me in the process. I'd say, "Hey, why don't you go home, change into some work clothes, and come back and get your hands dirty. I've got lots of stuff you could be doing to help me."

What would your response be?

A request like that would just take our relationship to a whole new level, wouldn't it? It's kind of like asking someone to help you move!

I'm guessing some of you would want to dive in and learn a little bit about how the whole sprinkler system works. Some of you would graciously decline my offer (and then slowly back away from the property).

But I'm guessing *none* of you would first decline my offer . . . and then go get a bunch of your friends, bring them to my driveway, and just stand around watching me do my work, commenting about what a great guy I am and what an incredible sprinkler system I've created.

I just don't think that would happen, but this is a little like what some of us are doing.

We've come to God's driveway. We've shown some interest in what He is doing. We've even complimented Him on how amazing everything looks and how great He is. But He's invited us into the process with him and would like us to help Him with the work. He's saying, "Why don't you get your work clothes on and jump in and help me? I'll teach you how I would do it and then let you get your hands dirty." Some of us have declined His offer, gone and gathered a bunch of our friends, and brought them back to the driveway to watch everything and continue to compliment Him on how amazing He is.

No matter who you are, no matter your age, because you are a member of humanity, you've been invited into the process of assisting in the assembly of this whole system to make it operate the way God would do it. Are you willing to jump in? Are you willing to get your hands dirty? Would you consider taking your relationship with God to a whole new level?

The biblical story tells us that Adam and Eve at first accepted this invitation and jumped right into the process with God in the garden. They were ruling, subduing, cultivating, and keeping. They were in their place doing their thing. But at some point, that changed. In simple terms, it was when they listened to someone other than the Master Gardener for direction regarding where to be and what to do. When that happened, humanity's rest ended and our representatives were exiled from Eden. Their experience then became an existence of pain and toil. To some degree this situation still exists today. Humanity is still trying to do what we were meant to do, but we are doing it under the authority of a different commander.

The Reminders Are Interconnected

God knew that humanity, after the fall and exile from the garden, would quickly forget that they had a place to be and a thing to do under God's rule. In the last chapter we discussed the "reminders of rest" that God put in place for the people of Israel. Let's briefly review what was presented:

1. First, God gave them weekly ways to practice and grow their faith (the gathering of manna and the fourth commandment).

2. Then He added several additional sabbath days to the yearly calendar (attached to the seven annual festivals of Passover, Unleavened Bread, First Fruits, Pentecost, Trumpets, Day of Atonement, and Tabernacles).

3. He then instructed people to experience an expanded idea of sabbath every seventh year (sabbatical year).

4. Every fiftieth year, they were to completely hit the reset button (the Year of Jubilee).

5. All these reminders of rest (their thing to do) were to be practiced in a land that God would provide (their place to be). If everything went well, this Promised Land would become known as a land of rest. The Israelites, living at rest with God, were supposed to be a reminder to all of humanity that the world had started out much differently than the curse-a-day world we now experience.

You might be tempted to see these restful reminders found in the Law of Moses as compartmentalized, stand-alone entities, meant to be evaluated individually. This is often how the Old Testament Law is explained, that it must be dissected into smaller segments so each part can be evaluated for its applicability to modern readers.[45] This compartmentalized type of study doesn't allow the interconnected nature of larger biblical themes to present themselves. It can mask those larger movements and bring thematic confusion to the process.

Many today who study the Bible are not taught to look for the larger themes that run throughout its stories and theology. I grew up studying the Bible in this compartmentalized way. As I studied Scripture, I learned many individual facts about God and how He works in the world, but even into early adulthood I hadn't pieced together many of the bigger thematic pictures.[46]

I call the way I used to study the "dot-to-dot method." In many ways it is very similar to those dot-to-dot pictures that are produced for children. Do you remember the last time you completed one of those? I remember having a whole book of dot-to-dots when I was young. In my childhood those pictures were always such a mystery, but as an adult, the pictures are pretty easy to figure out. What's the difference?

Adults look at those pictures and are able to quickly take in the whole page. They see the first set of dots in the rough outline of a dog. Then they notice another set that will become a bone, and over in the corner there's a set that will form a water dish that already says "Fido" on it! For adults who have been trained to look at the whole picture, there is no question about what's about to go down on the page.

But as a child I didn't have that same perspective. I'd look at the page, see a bunch of mysterious dots, and immediately get laser-focused on finding the number "one." This is what I was taught to do and I knew that's where everything should get started. Once I found the "one," I'd place my pencil on the page and then make my way to "two," "three," and so on. Then when I had made my way to the last number—and not really much before that—I'd allow my gaze to back away from the page and discover that the larger picture had magically appeared as I was connecting the individual points. That's when I'd realize for the first time, "It's a puppy!"

In a similar way, the Bible presents a theological dot-to-dot about God and how He created the universe to work. We sometimes get too laser-focused on the individual dots and miss the larger way they are interconnected. But when we are able to connect the individual points, we see truths that the larger themes offer.

For instance, consider when God gave the manna in the wilderness and instituted the sabbath observance (Exodus 16). We often study that story and see it as an end, in and of itself. Just one dot on the page. But shortly after that instance, Moses and the people arrive at Mount Sinai (Exodus 19) and then receive the Ten Commandments, including the fourth commandment of sabbath rest (Exodus 20). These could just be viewed as additional individual dots, but we are not supposed to interpret these "reminders of rest" as separate entities that functioned in and of themselves. The original audience understood each of these points on a continuum as part of a connected and expanding theology of rest. The process of rethinking what the Bible has to say about rest demands that we arrange the dots on this topic in the way the original readers understood them to be connected. When we do, a much larger—and more complex—picture of rest develops.

The Year of Jubilee Reframed

There are aspects of the Year of Jubilee that might help illustrate this interconnectedness. I've suggested that the jubilee year is the culmination of several reminders of rest in the Law of Moses. Every fiftieth year, one time for each generation, there was supposed to be this special Jubilee reminder of how things used to be, and a hope of a future time of rest.

This reset was not just a chance to remember the way things were fifty years prior, or even a reminder of the Israelites' entrance into the land under Joshua's leadership. It was intended to be a small glimpse of God's rule in Eden, and all the reminders in the progression leading up to the jubilee were interconnected with it. There's a description of this connection in the text:

You are also to count off seven sabbaths of years for yourself, seven times seven years, so that you have the time of the seven sabbaths of years, namely, forty-nine years. You shall then sound a ram's horn abroad on the tenth day of the seventh month: on the day of atonement, you shall sound a horn all through your land. You shall thus consecrate the fiftieth year and proclaim a release through the land to all its inhabitants. It shall be a jubilee for you, and each of you shall return to his own property, and each of you shall return to his family. (Leviticus 25:8–10)

This passage describes how the people of Israel were to begin the Year of Jubilee. On the tenth day of the seventh month, they were to sound a horn. Why is this important? In the Jewish calendar, that particular day is a sabbath day attached to one of the yearly national festivals, the Day of Atonement (Leviticus 23:26–32). The jubilee horn, which signified the beginning of the Year of Jubilee, was to be blown on the Day of Atonement. It was on this yearly festival sabbath that the nation pushed another reset button, the yearly forgiveness of the nation's sins. The Day of Atonement was also the only day of fasting within Judaism.[47] The people fasted in anticipation of God's provision.

The highlight of the Day of Atonement festival was the offering of two goats on behalf of the nation. The priests brought both goats to the temple on that day. One of the goats was sacrificed, and its blood was taken and sprinkled on the mercy seat on top of the ark of the covenant. But the other goat wasn't killed. This second goat was called the "scapegoat." The high priest would place his hands on the head of this goat (symbolizing the transfer of the nation's sin onto the animal). Then do you know what they did? They sent the goat out to the wilderness, never to be seen again.[48] It was a very vivid picture of the removal of sins from the people.

On this one day, God's "telescope" of rest reminders seemed to collapse upon itself and converged into a unique, multifaceted picture of rest. Let's put our pencils on the page and connect all the dots.

1. The jubilee year began with the blowing of a trumpet.

2. It was the beginning of the yearly Day of Atonement festival.

3. It was the beginning of a second consecutive sabbath year.

4. It was a sabbath day.

5. People fasted in anticipation of God's provision.

6. Two goats were brought to the temple.

7. The blood of one entered the Holy of Holies.

8. The sins on the scapegoat were taken away.[49]

9. The relationship with God was restored.

10. Food was made available for everyone.

11. It was a reminder of God's rule and order for the cosmos.

12. Land was returned to its original owners and remained at rest.

13. All bondslaves were granted unconditional freedom.

14. It was the beginning of a special year in the Promised Land, a place of rest.[50]

With all of these elements connected, God's picture of rest is complete. Now that we've connected all the dots, let's back away from the page, give it a quarter turn, and see the picture we've created. . . . It's a hammock!

Wait a minute, that's not right! We must have turned the picture the wrong way. When we flip it and look at it, right side up, we notice the depiction of a special garden on top of a mountain. And as we might expect, there's God right at the center, ensuring that the picture of rest is complete.

The beginning of the jubilee year was a dramatic reminder of what it was like for Adam and Eve to follow God's rule in Eden. It was a reminder of a time when there was no sin, everyone had their place and their thing, nobody was in debt, there were no poor, no rich—everybody was just doing what they were supposed to be doing.

The individual components of rest were never meant to be understood as stand-alone entities. When we understand the individual pictures, and how they are interconnected within the entire theology, we are able to realize the complexity of the larger picture the dots create.

It's also through this larger perspective we realize just how insufficient those interconnected Old Testament reminders were. You would think, given the specific instructions within the Mosaic Law, that Israel would have been incredibly diligent to make sure everything happened exactly as it was supposed to. But Israel's practice of these reminders was, at best, inconsistent. They sometimes went decades without observing any of them. The reminders were good but they were insufficient, in and of themselves, to return true rest to the creation.

Prophetic Corrections and Hope

This truth became more apparent as the prophets brought God's message to the people. Prophets would always bring a message of judgment and hope. The judgment was God's response to the people's unwillingness to live under His rule and authority, and the hope was for the future.

The book of Isaiah includes an example of this type of prophetic message. In Isaiah 58, the prophet first brings a message of correction to the people of Israel about how they had misunderstood and misapplied several aspects of the jubilee year. The chapter begins with God's direction for the prophet to sound his voice like a trumpet (v. 1). Isaiah then used that voice to correct the people's practice of fasting (vv. 4–5) and described God's true fast where the oppressed are freed from wickedness and supplied all their needs (vv. 6–7).

The chapter ends with Isaiah presenting the clearest Old Testament picture of God's expectation of the sabbath. How were they to observe the sabbath? What type of activities were the people to cease? Let's read the words of Isaiah directly:

If because of the sabbath, you turn your foot from doing your own pleasure on My holy day, and call the sabbath a delight, the holy day of the LORD honorable, and honor it, desisting from your own ways, from seeking your own pleasure and speaking your own word. Then you will take delight in the LORD, and I will make you ride on the heights of the earth; and I will feed you with the heritage of Jacob your father, for the mouth of the LORD has spoken. (Isaiah 58:13–14)

That's just about as clear a definition as the Bible provides for the sabbath. It's a day where we are to honor God by walking away from our own attempts to order the world in our own way. We are to cease and desist seeking our own pleasure and speaking our own words toward our own glory. It's a day of denial. We deny our will and submit to the will of the one who made us, the one who knows us better than we know ourselves.

Those are the words of the Lord through Isaiah the prophet to a group of people who had misunderstood the reason for sabbath, fasting, the Day of Atonement, the sabbatical year, and the Year of Jubilee. Perhaps it's also a word of correction for us, we who have also misunderstood and misapplied several aspects of godly rest.

But correction is never the end of the prophet's statement. Isaiah's message ends with the hope of a day where humanity will "ride on the heights of the earth." While I'm not sure exactly what that will look like—it sure sounds exceedingly fun and exciting! It's the promise of better days ahead.

The prophets' messages of hope often spoke of one who would come, who would be able to solve the problem of humanity's exile. The Law, the Prophets, and the Writings (the whole Old Testament) continually present that humanity should be expecting something better than the reminders of rest. Something more capable of bringing rest back to the creation.

Remember our message from earlier in Hebrews 4:

For if Joshua had given them rest, He would not have spoken of another day after that. So there remains a Sabbath rest for the people of God. For the one who has entered His rest has himself also rested from his works, as God did from His. Therefore, let us be diligent to enter that rest, so that no one will fall, through following the same example of disobedience. (Hebrews 4:8–11)

If it was the Old Testament character of Joshua who had given Israel true rest, the prophets would not have given the hope of another day after that. So, God expects us to read the Old Testament story and emerge expecting a better offer of rest than the reminders could extend. The reminders were significant in their original setting, but we are not supposed to be satisfied with any of them individually—or even all of them collectively. We are to see them and think about a lost reality that existed before, in Eden, and expect that one day that restful existence will be restored and fully realized in the new creation.

The Shadow World

The New Testament describes the Old Testament Law, and some of the reminders of rest within the Law, as shadows. So, let's talk about shadows a little and look into the first century's cultural context of this ancient description.

I like to think of a shadow as a flat, one-dimensional, colorless representation of a substance that has a full set of dimensions, color, and mass. To be sure, shadows reflect aspects of the substance that casts them. For instance, suppose I was standing in front of you with our two mini Schnauzers, Tank and Lady, on leads next to me with the sun at my back. Now suppose you were only able to see the shadows that the dogs and I cast on the ground. You would likely be able to tell that there is a person and two dogs standing before you. You might not know it was me specifically, but you could hopefully tell it was a person. You might not be able to tell they were mini Schnauzers, but you could probably tell they were small dogs. Shadows are able to represent a general description of a substance, but they are never able to share all the details of the substance that casts them.

Shadows in Philosophy

There once was a philosopher by the name of Plato. Maybe you've heard of him? Plato was one of the most important figures in Western philosophy. He introduced several new ideas to the philosophic world of his day, but many of his ideas were built on the foundations of those who preceded him. He interacted with, and further developed, the ideas of philosophers like Heraclitus and Socrates. To give some historical perspective, Plato lived about four hundred years before the time of Jesus, but well after the events of the Old Testament had concluded. Many of the questions he investigated are still being discussed today, and his ideas continue to have a profound impact on Christian thinking.[51]

For Plato, the "good life" depended on a well-ordered soul. He described the human purpose as one of moving from a state of interior disorder to one of order. This process entailed the moderation of life's passions through one's reason and will. His was the struggle to regulate the three parts of the soul with virtuous responses to human passions. Plato described this as a conflict that each individual waged largely by themselves. I find it interesting that even secular philosophy recognized the innate human desire to bring order to chaotic situations. It also recognized that struggle begins with the human soul.

Around 380 BC, Plato wrote his work *The Republic*. In this book, he discusses an idea that he calls the "world of the forms." For Plato, a form was the nonphysical "ideal version" of something in an unseen realm. He argued that thinking about the ideal version of things is one of the most useful exercises we can have. From his perspective, these forms exist as a blueprint in an unseen world, but they cast shadows into the physical world in which we live. So, platonically speaking, we don't have "forms" in our world, but we do have shadows of the unseen ideal forms.

Here's an example: Let's take the idea of "good." There exists an ideal good, but when we talk about "good" we are usually forced to think of it in terms of an "example of good" that we know of or have experienced here on earth.

"Do you know Sally? She is a good person."

"Wow, that ice cream was good."

"Good dog!"

While these are examples of "good" and certainly bring out different aspects of its meaning, do any of these truly give examples of the Platonic "ideal good?"

While Sally might be a "good person," she certainly has times where she is looking out for her best interests.

That "good ice cream" has too many calories.

That "good dog" pooped on my neighbor's lawn. (OK, maybe that *is* the ideal good!)

When we see "examples of good" on Earth, we get a glimpse of "ideal good"—but it's only a shadow of good. Plato suggests that beyond all the shadows of good that we know and experience, there is an unadulterated ideal good that is better than anything we have experienced in this world.

Plato's Cave

Plato explains some of these ideas in a very famous story, usually referred to as the "allegory of the cave."[52] I'd like to describe it for illustrative purposes.

Plato asked us to imagine a group of ordinary individuals who have become prisoners in an underground cave. They are completely fastened to chairs with their heads in vices so they can only look straight ahead. They've been this way since they were born. In front of them is the wall of the cave in which they've lived their entire life.

Behind them is a fire, and between the people and the fire is a walkway with others passing by holding up different objects. The fire casts its light on the objects and in turn casts a shadow on the cave wall in front of the people. But the people don't have any concept of what's going on behind them, because they've never been able to turn around and see what's happening. All they ever get to see is the shadows on the wall in front of them. The shadows are their whole world.

Plato suggests that the people in this fixed condition, with their limited understanding of reality, would eventually begin to think that the shadows on the wall in front of them were something in and of themselves. They would begin to notice characteristics of the different shadows. They would start to name the shadows and study them. Eventually, without the benefit of any other perspective, they would begin to think that the shadows were actually the substance that was casting them.

This is an allegory that Plato used to describe the process of education. Those strapped into the chairs are the people in the world who are not aware of his world of the forms and who rely on the philosopher's clarity of perspective to explain the true nature of reality. Plato suggests that oftentimes we in the world look at things that we think are real, but are only shadows which reflect a much more complex unseen ideal.

Plato's cave allegory was inserted into the Greek philosophic discussion shortly before Alexander the Great conquered a large portion of the world. Alexander's conquests allowed Greek to become a standard language of commerce. This standardization of language allowed thoughts and ideas to spread much more rapidly than ever before.[53] Philosophers who followed Plato interacted with his thoughts and further developed ideas about the world of the forms, but it was Alexander's exploits that allowed that philosophic conversation to take root throughout the known world.

It's into that secular philosophic background, nearly four hundred years after Plato lived, that Jesus of Nazareth was born. And some of the authors of the New Testament seem to borrow imagery from the secular philosophic thought of their day to describe the truth of the God of the Bible. The authors of the New Testament don't just present Jesus in terms of Jewish thoughts and history; they also explain Him in terms the secular philosophic world of their day would have easily recognized and understood.[54] It makes sense why they would do this. Who, besides Jewish people, would need to come to believe in this Christ character?

Oh yeah: the Gentiles would!

The average Gentile didn't have an extensive understanding of Jewish history and culture. So it's not surprising that the New Testament authors, well versed in both Jewish and Greek cultures, reached into their multicultural bag of analogies and presented Jesus in terms that all the people of the world, both Jew and Gentile, would understand.

New Testament Mentions of Shadows

Two books in the New Testament specifically present the Law of Moses as a precursor of something much better that exists in the heavenly realm. In the books of Hebrews and Colossians, the Law of Moses and the ministry it details are described as shadows. These references to shadows certainly include the idea of foreshadowing something that was to come in the future. But they also include the specific nuance that the Law is a tangible representation of something that exists in the unseen spiritual realm. The author of Hebrews mentions this idea twice. The first describes Jesus as a priest whose position is unlike the Levites who served under the Law of Moses.

> Now if He (Jesus) were on earth, He would not be a priest at all, since there are those who offer the gifts according to the Law; who serve a copy and shadow of the heavenly things. (Hebrews 8:4–5a)

This passage suggests the Old Testament Levitical priesthood served a shadow ministry. It was an earthly ministry that portrayed another ministry happening in the heavenly realm, which is Jesus's priesthood. The second mention of the Law's shadow ministry is found just a couple of chapters later in Hebrews 10:

> For the Law, since it has only a shadow of the good things to come and not the very form of things, can never, by the same sacrifices which they offer continually year by year, make perfect those who draw near. (Hebrews 10:1)

These two passages suggest that the summative purpose of the Law of Moses was to shadow a heavenly ministry that would be fully realized at a later date. They suggest that the heavenly ministry would not only surpass the Law but truly explain the reason it ever existed.

The third New Testament mention of the shadow ministry of the Law is found in the second chapter of Paul's letter to the Colossians. This chapter begins by commenting on how humanity was caught in the death grip of sin, but that Jesus saved us from that condition. It says Jesus, on the cross, "cancelled out the certificate of debt" attached to humanity (Colossians 2:14).

Did you notice the terminology that the author used? It says that there was a situation of debt that humanity had—but that debt has been cancelled. This should sound slightly familiar. It is supposed to remind you of the Year of Jubilee, when all debts were released. But that might be a backward way of looking at the theology of the passage. It's not that Jesus's ministry was a preview of the jubilee year. Jesus's ministry is the end goal; His ministry is what the Old Testament release of debts was prefiguring.

The message of the Old Testament is that humanity was outside of God's rule and order (dead in transgressions), but that Christ has reestablished the proper rule and order for humanity to follow (made you alive together with Him). Having reversed the curse of the garden, He has stripped all other rulers and authorities of the position they usurped from God. It's this discussion of the cross events that builds to the argument leading to our "shadow" passage in Colossians 2:

> Therefore no one is to act as your judge in regard to food or drink or in respect to a festival or a new moon or a Sabbath day—things which are a mere shadow of what is to come; but the substance belongs to Christ. (Colossians 2:16–17)

Here's my paraphrase of that passage: "Hey New Testament believer, based on the cancelled debt and the victory of Christ spoken of earlier, no one is now able to judge you in regard to the following things found in the Old Testament Law: how to eat, when and where to gather for worship, and other ritual items that regulate the rhythms of life. Those things are mere shadows of a greater ministry. The substance that casts those shadows is Jesus."

This passage from Colossians prompts us to look back into the Old Testament (and specifically the ministry of the things mentioned) and see shadows, or a vague outline, which represents the ministry of the substance. Colossians tells us that Jesus is that substance. The full meaning of those shadow ministries can only be found in Him. In other words, Jesus is the Shadow-Caster.

Is the Church in a Cave?

As I understand a bit more about Plato's cave and see how Paul and the author of Hebrews may have interacted with those ideas, I wonder if some people in the church today might be similar to those people in Plato's cave. Let me explain.

I think we in the church sometimes interact with things that are shadows—aspects of the Old Testament Law that Scripture has clearly defined as shadows (as we've just seen in Hebrews 8:4–5; 10:1; Colossians 2:16–17)—but may have come to think of them as having their own substance, as an ideal form. I believe this misunderstanding has contributed to our confusion regarding biblical rest.

The Old Testament shadows are not the substance. They were only ever meant to act as a flat, one-dimensional reminder of something else. They should only be pointing us toward the Shadow-Caster. Jesus is the only one with theological form and substance.

Plato came to an interesting conclusion in his analogy of the cave. He wrote *The Republic* as a dialogue between characters. One of those characters explains what it would be like to live in a world like the cave where people were trapped only seeing the shadows. That character suggests eventually groups of people would form and these groups would begin to be "governed by men who fight over shadows with one another and form factions for the sake of ruling, as though it were some great good."[55]

But in reality, that's not the form of the good.

I feel like this is where many people are in their understanding of sabbath rest. The church has been arguing with one another for years over how to define and interpret the shadows of rest. These disagreements have caused us to form factions; as if the shadow is the substance. There are people who are looking square on at all the sabbaths prescribed in the Mosaic Law and are unaware they are only looking at a shadow.

But in reality, that's not the true form of the good. In gospel terms, what's the form of the good? Who is the substance that cast all the Old Testament shadows?

It's Jesus.[56]

The longer we, as a group of believers, choose to focus on the shadow and talk about and discuss and argue about the shadow, the longer we are not really acknowledging that there is a Substance that this whole thing is about.

If there's one idea we should take away from this discussion, it's that the whole of the New Testament presents Jesus as "the thing." He's it. Everything before Him pointed to Him. If we're not talking about Jesus in terms of His ministry fulfilling all the shadows of the Old Testament, we're missing the boat. New Testament believers should not be looking to the Old Testament shadows of rest as the solution for unrest. Rather, we should be focusing on Jesus as the fulfillment of those ideas. The shadows should always guide us to their intended end.

I know the question this brings to the table. It's the elephant-in-the-room question that a book about rest must eventually address. Here it is:

If Jesus is the One who offers true rest, what role do the Old Testament shadows play today?

There are many ideas about how to answer this question, so this is where it might feel like I'm stepping on someone's toes a bit. You likely have some well-established beliefs and long-practiced patterns entrenched in your life around these ideas. In later chapters, I'll share my thoughts in detail, but I think we need to wrestle with the question a little longer. This is the crux of the issue for our time. How are we to interact with the shadows? So to acknowledge the elephant question: for now, please allow me to evasively answer with another question—or maybe five:

> If the Old Testament shadows were there to help humanity anticipate and understand the ministry of Jesus, can they still do that today?
>
> Can modern believers interact with the sabbath shadows without getting stuck in cul-de-sacs?
>
> What does it mean to live at rest under Jesus's rule and authority?
>
> How do we experience sabbath rest in Jesus?
>
> What does it mean for Jesus to be the fulfillment of these things?

The answers to these questions can, in part, be found in the stories and theology of the four Gospels. Those accounts show us Jesus—a human living at rest with God, but One who is also the visible expression of that invisible God (Colossians 1:15). He is the hope about which the prophets of the Old Testament spoke. When we read about how Jesus lived his life, and are able to put His words back into their original context, we can understand what it means for humanity to truly live at rest. So, to the Gospels we go, to see how Jesus interacted with and offered rest to those He met.

ADDITIONAL

REST

RESOURCES

CHAPTER 4

THE FULFILLMENT OF REST

Imagine the following movie scene. The hero of the story has learned a tough life lesson. It's a lesson that may have made him or her into a social outcast. But this character gets a chance, in one scene near the end of the movie, to make a dramatic statement to all the other characters. It's a statement communicated through conquering a difficult situation, or maybe a powerful speech. When the outcast makes their point, a silence falls upon those who are present; it's a collective pause to give everyone time to process what just happened. Then you hear it.

A single clap . . .

Then another clap . . . and a third.

Eventually a second person joins along with the first. Then a few others begin clapping too. The tension of the scene suddenly breaks and everyone, including even the movie's skeptical antagonist, joins in as the speed and intensity of the clapping increases. And you, watching the movie, fight back a tear from your eye as you share in the profoundness of this overly dramatic and very scripted moment.

You've just experienced a "slow clap" scene.[57]

These types of scenes were particularly popular in 1980s high school movies when the "nerds," who have been bullied for the entire movie by the "cool athletes," finally stand up and defend themselves.[58] You may remember a slow-clap scene was the defining moment in *Rudy*, when he returned to the football practice squad after wanting to quit. But likely the best slow-clap example was in *Cool Runnings*, when the Olympic Jamaican bobsled team carried their broken sled across the finish line after a dramatic crash. (I probably should have given a spoiler alert for that one!)

Slow-clap scenes are times of unusual social clarity.

When you think about the ministry of Jesus, you might wonder if He ever had a slow-clap moment. To be sure, He was a social outcast who profoundly brought clarity to His culture. You might remember the drama He created when He reshaped people's understanding through dramatic teaching. Or the times He unhinged the laws of nature by healing the sick or walking on water. It could be argued that Jesus's whole time on earth was one significant slow-clap moment that brought unusual clarity to the entire world!

But to my knowledge, no one ever slow-clapped for Jesus.

What is interesting to see is how Jesus brought this type of social clarity to His culture's understanding of sabbath rest. In several stories, Jesus interacts with the theme of rest as He proclaims the coming of His kingdom. We will examine a few of these instances. From these gospel snippets, we'll see not only how Jesus challenged the errant thinking of His day but also how He invites us to do the same in ours. So let's cast our gaze into the gospel accounts of the ministry of the Shadow-Caster and examine how Jesus interacted with biblical rest.

What Does It Mean to Fulfill?

In the last chapter we discussed how several parts of the Old Testament storyline included prophetic previews of Jesus's ministry. Along those lines, it shouldn't be surprising to find that when Jesus arrived, He often referred back to that ancient storyline that predicted He would come.

There are many places where the New Testament authors let us know that Jesus did something in fulfillment of an Old Testament prophecy,[59] and there are a few times when Jesus himself made these connections. For us to understand His relationship with rest, we should first clarify what it means for Jesus to "fulfill" something from the Old Testament.

One such teaching is found in Matthew 5:17, where Jesus said, "Do not think that I came to abolish the Law or the Prophets; I did not come to abolish but to fulfill."

Let's look more closely at what Jesus said. He specifically mentioned the "Law" and the "Prophets" when He spoke. But sometimes in our modern context, we like to drop "the Prophets" from His statement and reduce it down to a passage that just concerns the "Law." But that's us trying to answer our own questions. We want to know what modern-day responsibilities believers might still have to the Old Testament Law. We wonder if Jesus is talking about just certain parts of the Law but not other parts. Could He be referring to just the Ten Commandments when he says "the Law"? Or maybe it's only the Ten Commandments that are upheld in the New Testament that He has "fulfilled." We often think of laws as a set of individual rules to follow, and we want to know which of those rules still might apply in our setting. At times, you too may have thought about the Old Testament Law in this segmented way.

But Jesus isn't speaking about the Law from that perspective. When He mentions "the Law and the Prophets," He's referring to His culture's understanding of these concepts. From a Jewish perspective, the Law refers to the teaching of the first five books of the Old Testament (Genesis, Exodus, Leviticus, Numbers, and Deuteronomy). It includes not just a set of rules to follow but the entire narrative of how God created and interacted with the world. This is very different than the way we think of individual laws in our modern setting.

Jesus also included the Prophets in the same sentence. The Old Testament Prophets, the actual people who communicated God's words, are obviously no longer around. They lived in the past, but we still have their teachings; and similar to the Law referring to the teaching of the first five books, in Jewish thought, the Prophets are a section of the Old Testament Scripture. This is what Jesus references in his statement. He's talking about the section of Scripture referred to as the Prophets.

What then would it mean to "fulfill the Prophets"? The Prophets bring a perspective about who God is, how He has defined the problem of sin, and what His ultimate solution to that problem is. The Prophets' presentation of these things is strategically interwoven into the same message presented in the Law. It's all the same story. So, we should consider the Law and the Prophets as two large sections of Scripture that contain the message of who God is and what His plan is to save the world. When we do this, we can properly frame what Jesus is saying.

I could paraphrase His statement this way: "I didn't come to get rid of the teaching found in the Old Testament Law and Prophets about who God is and His plan for humanity. I'm not here to get rid of that teaching or change that plan. The Law and the Prophets were ultimately talking about Me and My ministry. I'm here to fulfill the long-awaited plan of salvation they spoke of."

We see this same distinction later in His ministry when Jesus says, "all things which are written about Me in the Law of Moses and the Prophets and the Psalms must be fulfilled" (Luke 24:44). Here Jesus refers to the Jewish three-part organization of the entire Old Testament: the Law, Prophets, and Writings.[60] So it's not just two-thirds of the Old Testament Scriptures (the Law and Prophets) that Jesus came to fulfill—it's really the whole thing (Law, Prophets, and Writings).

Jesus saw the whole of the Old Testament as an interconnected prequel that led up to His arrival. He invites us to read it in the same way. He didn't come to get rid of, or further segment, that message. His ministry is the fulfillment of the whole Old Testament.

Jesus's Mic-Drop Moment

Slow claps are not the only way we've learned to emphasize moments of social clarity in our modern culture. You may have recently seen a performer, at the end of an impressive speech or presentation, drop their microphone on the ground and walk off the stage. It's a phenomenon that, obviously, has only been around since the creation of the microphone. But these theatrical "mic-drop" moments have developed into a (potentially expensive) form of punctuation in our modern day. Some people use them as an expression of triumph, when a particularly impressive point has been made.

You might be wondering if Jesus ever had a "mic-drop" moment during His life. There is one story, near the beginning of His public ministry in his small hometown of Nazareth, when Jesus had the ultimate mic-drop moment. He claimed to be the fulfillment of all the ritual symbolism to which the Old Testament reminders of rest pointed.

The story is in Luke 4, where we find Jesus teaching in the synagogue. He got up from his seat and was handed the scroll of Isaiah. Then He found the place where it said,

> "The Spirit of the Lord is upon me, because he anointed me to preach the gospel to the poor. He has sent me to proclaim release to the captives, and recovery of sight to the blind. To set free those who are oppressed, to proclaim the favorable year of the Lord." And He closed the book, gave it back to the attendant and sat down; the eyes of all in the synagogue were fixed on Him. And He began to say to them, "Today this Scripture has been fulfilled in your hearing." (Luke 4:18–21)

Then what happened? It doesn't say it in the text, but I can just picture Jesus standing up, dropping His ancient microphone on the dirt floor of the synagogue in Nazareth, and saying, "Messiah out!"

Why would I suggest this is one such grand and dramatic moment? First, this all happens on a seventh-day sabbath. It's not by chance that on one of these shadowy days of rest Jesus claimed to usher in a new age by quoting an Isaiah passage referring to the ultimate Year of Jubilee.[61] How do we know that Jesus was claiming an ultimate Jubilee? Well, the text He reads from the prophet Isaiah gives us some clues. The prophets would often speak of concepts from the Mosaic Law not just as ways to remember how God dealt with humanity in the past, but also as hopeful clues for what God would do in the future. Isaiah does this with the Year of Jubilee. He takes the idea of release from slavery, an idea from Israel's past, and links it to a future release for all of humanity—the fulfillment of the concept. Consider these parts of the passage:

"*. . . to preach the gospel to the poor.*" "Gospel" means "good news." Jesus suggests that He has been anointed to bring good news to the poor. What is good news if you are poor? The fact that you're not poor anymore! It's good news to hear that your debts have been cancelled and that you are on even ground with everyone else in life. That's what was to happen in the Year of Jubilee . . . the big financial reset button.

But Isaiah takes this idea and moves it past the Old Testament financial metaphor and into the spiritual fulfillment of that concept. When Jesus reads the prophet's passage, He isn't talking about paying off peoples' financial obligations. His good news deals with the cancelling of humanity's debt in regard to sin and unrest.

"*. . . to proclaim release to the captives.*" In the Hebrew text, the word used for "release" in Isaiah is the same one used in Leviticus 25:10 to describe the "release" announced to all the inhabitants of Israel at the beginning of the Year of Jubilee.

So, what is a Jubilee release of "captives?" Captives of what? Again, Isaiah was both looking back to the release from financial slavery offered in the Year of Jubilee and forward to the fulfillment of this concept. And like Isaiah, Jesus had much more than financial freedom on His mind. He was speaking of His ministry of releasing people from their slavery to sin. He's saying, "All those who find themselves captive to sin, I'm here to negotiate your release from that situation."

"*. . . to proclaim the favorable year of the Lord.*" What is this favorable year? This is yet another link to the Year of Jubilee, the culmination of all the "rest shadows" we have followed in the Law. It is the year where everything resets back to a picture of humanity living at rest in an Edenic existence with God. It's Isaiah who looks forward to the ultimate fulfillment of that idea, and Jesus attached Himself to that vision.

"*Today this scripture has been fulfilled*[62] *in your hearing.*" There's that "fulfilled" language again. Let's remind ourselves what it means to fulfill. Jesus isn't saying he's trying to abolish or get rid of the Old Testament concept of Jubilee. He is claiming to fulfill the entire plan of salvation that the Old Testament reminders of rest typified and foreshadowed; the ultimate plan to return all creation to rest with God.[63] Jesus said He came to fulfill that plan, and then announced humanity's release from the long-standing curse.

After this mic-drop moment in Nazareth, Jesus continued in His public ministry. At several points, He took advantage of opportunities to further elaborate and clarify exactly what He meant that day in Nazareth, and how His fulfillment of Jubilee would completely change the way people understood and practiced rest. We will now look at an extended section in Matthew's gospel where Jesus does exactly that.

Jesus Offered Rest

I shared earlier that my first "real adult job" was teaching junior high English. As a young teacher, I was introduced to various theories regarding the different ways people learn. I was told that some students are predominantly visual learners who would retain material better when it's attached to a visual representation of information (like a chart, map, or picture). I was also told that other students are auditory learners and remember information best through sounds (like listening to a podcast, or presenting information through a song). Some students connect best through reading and writing (like studying from a textbook or composing an essay). Still others learn best with kinesthetic movement (like walking around or tapping a pencil).

These learning styles were popularized in teaching circles by the acronym VARK (Visual, Auditory, Reading/writing, Kinesthetic). And eventually a student questionnaire was developed to help determine a student's best "learning style." Educators theorized they could reach every student, even those who struggled to learn, by tailoring their instruction to match each student's preferred learning style.[64]

Even though Jesus, the teacher, didn't have the VARK questionnaire in mind when He taught about sabbath rest, it's interesting to notice the variety of ways He presented information to His first-century audience. Sometimes He referred back to the ancient words of the Jewish scriptures (reading/writing). At other times He instructed as people walked with Him from one place to another (kinesthetic). Sometimes a physical healing (visual) helped attract people's attention, allowing them to more deeply understand His lessons.

With that in mind, we now turn our attention to Matthew 11:25–12:14, a passage where Jesus incorporates several learning styles in His teaching on rest. In this text, Matthew packages four examples that display what Jesus's fulfillment of the Jubilee really means. These stories also highlight just how misguided the understanding of biblical rest had become.

In Jesus's day the sabbath had been hijacked by the religious leaders. Instead of being a mechanism to move people toward God's rule, the leaders used the sabbath to become taskmasters over the people. Proper seventh-day sabbath observance had become a very confusing and polarizing topic. But as we will see, Jesus seemed to be less concerned with preserving a misunderstood shadow ministry and more focused on the larger biblical theme of rest. This is first illustrated in Jesus's offer of rest in Matthew 11:25–30:

> Come to Me, all who are weary and heavy-laden, and I will give you rest. Take My yoke upon you and learn from Me for I am gentle and humble in heart, and you will find rest for your souls. For My yoke is easy and My burden is light. (Matthew 11:28–30)

The Jewish culture already had a fully developed concept of spiritual rest. Those who heard Jesus say these words would have been familiar with many Old Testament passages that portray God as the one who is able to offer rest to His people (Exodus 33:12–15; Deuteronomy 3:18–20; Joshua 1:13; 21:44; Jeremiah 50:34; Ezekiel 34:15). Jesus's statement assumes a familiarity with this extended context. The people would have understood, and so should we, that Jesus claimed to be in a role that previously had only been associated with God. So, this is quite a statement He makes.

Let's also notice what Jesus is *not* saying. He doesn't offer a better definition of a one-day-a-week break from humanity's work under the curse. One day a week is a shadow offering. Jesus's offer was complete rest, the full concept, the fulfillment of the idea. He claimed to be the cure for humanity's unrest and rebellion against God.

A Yoke of Rest

> Take My yoke upon you and learn from Me ... for my yoke is easy and My burden is light. (Matthew 11:29–30)

Most of us, even though we've never used one ourselves, probably already know what a yoke is. It's that farming implement which, when fastened over the necks of two animals, allows them to work together to pull a plow or cart. The problem is, that's the extent of knowledge I have about yokes. Let's be honest, I really know nothing about their practical use. And that's a problem, because to understand Jesus's statement I need to know more than I do about yokes. I decided to look into it a little more and find out how the term is used in the Bible.

What I found surprised me.

Biblically speaking, a yoke seems to have more to do with who's controlling the reins of the implement than whatever is attached to it. The farmer who holds the reins is the one who controls what work the yoked animals are to do. This relationship is highlighted in the story of Rehoboam's succession of his father, King Solomon (2 Chronicles 10). Shortly after Solomon died, people came to Rehoboam using the following yoke metaphor,

Your father (King Solomon) made our yoke hard; now therefore lighten the hard service of your father and his heavy yoke which he put on us, and we will serve you. (2 Chronicles 10:4)

In this example, King Solomon's yoke was not the one to which he was attached as a worker, but rather the one to which he held the reins. Solomon was the one controlling what work the people (those under his yoke) were to do. In turn, Rehoboam did not listen to the people's request and responded,

Whereas my father loaded you with a heavy yoke, I will add to your yoke. (2 Chronicles 10:11)

Needless to say, this insensitive response was the beginning of the end for Israel's united kingdom.

In another Old Testament passage, the prophet Jeremiah presents God's offer of rest together with the metaphor of being "yoked" to a master. Jeremiah suggested that the Israelites could either be yoked to God, and fall under His rule and authority, or be yoked to the bonds of pagan worship (Jeremiah 2:20; 5:4). Even though the Israelites had, time and time again, chosen to devote themselves to the yoke of pagan gods, God had always hoped they would find their rest by trusting in His rule and authority.

We might be tempted to think we are free to do what we want in life. But the Bible suggests that it's not a decision of "personal freedom" versus being "attached to a yoke." In the biblical worldview, humanity is always attached to a yoke. The question is: Whose yoke do you choose? Is it the one that makes you work in opposition to God's direction, or the one that leads you to the place you're supposed to be and allows you to work the way you're supposed to?

In the biblical setting, the yoke metaphor can also describe the type of work done while attached to the implement. What do I mean? Jesus says His yoke is "easy" or "pleasant." A farming implement can't be "easy." A yoke can be "wooden," "smooth," or "full of slivers" . . . but it can't be "easy." "Easy," then, must refer to the work done while attached to the yoke. Jesus says the work we do, when properly paired with Him, is what's easy. He's contrasting that with the work done apart from Him, yoked to the Edenic curse (Genesis 3:16–19). When humanity is attached to the yoke of the curse, the work is heavy and painfully unpleasant.

Jesus also doesn't suggest that His rest is inactivity without responsibility. In fact, it's exactly the opposite. Jesus's offer of rest is directly linked to the work of His yoke. Notice the progression of His argument:

I will give you rest. (v. 28)

Take my yoke. (v. 29)

You will find rest for your souls. (v. 29)

For my yoke is easy . . . (v. 30)

For Jesus, rest is an instrument of work. Or, maybe we could say the inverse of that: Jesus's work is an instrument of rest. Work and rest are the same thing? That seems like an oxymoron when we insert our modern definitions of those concepts. We ask, "How is it that work can be rest?" In Jesus's kingdom, things are often upside down from the way we think they are (and thank God they are).

Jesus offers the ability to be yoked (to do your work) attached to Him, and to do your work while learning from Him. It's a work that, when you are doing it, seems comfortable and natural because you are attached to the One who created you for that work. It's what you were made to do, and being yoked to Jesus is the method in which you were always supposed to do it.[65]

But Jesus is able to offer something that wasn't available in the Old Testament. In this metaphor, Jesus claims to be the God who holds the reins that lead to rest. In addition to that role, when Jesus became a human He uniquely joined with humanity and became yoked alongside us. It's a truly beautiful picture of the incarnation. Jesus is the one pulling the reins leading those under His yoke, and at the same time He is the human yoked right alongside us, explaining to us why the reins are pulling in that direction. What a beautiful picture that explains so much about how Jesus fulfills these concepts!

This is how Jesus is able to say, "learn from me, for I am gentle and humble in heart." It's in the person of Jesus that we have One walking right alongside us. He experienced the joys and disappointments of the curse-a-day world the same way we do. We don't have to turn all the way around to see who's got the reins. We can just turn our head to the side and follow His lead.

There's much more we could learn about yokes, but we now understand enough to make this idea a practical part of our everyday lives. Yet, most of us would still be completely useless in a barnyard.

How ironic.

Practical Yoke Application

Before we move on in the Matthew passage, let's move out of the theological for a moment and ask a very practical question: What did God create each of us to do? You probably already have a good idea what some of your gifts and talents might be, but you may not have considered how you could use those talents as an act of sabbath worship. Please hear me, I don't just mean on a Sunday or Wednesday in a church building. Those opportunities are certainly part of the picture, but Jesus presents opportunities to follow His lead every day of the week. When we take His yoke upon us, the idea is that God will intentionally lead us into everyday situations that offer rest.

What would it look like for you to fully step under Jesus's yoke? How could today change if He were the one in charge of that relationship? Where would He take you? What would His yoke have you doing? The answers to these questions could have long-term ramifications, but for now let's just consider today. How can you experience sabbath rest today?

You might need to change plans and shift what you do. You may need to change why you do it. It might be nothing more than expecting God to lead you into situations you wouldn't necessarily choose on your own but that you are uniquely gifted to handle.

In fact, God may have already put you in contact with a new way to use your gifts and talents. Someone might even be waiting to hear back from you about your willingness to step into a new situation. Are you willing to go down those roads and see where they lead? Each of us have opportunities right in front of us today that will lead us right down Sabbath Street, and into His fully developed neighborhood of rest.

I invite you to take a minute, before reading on, to further consider these things and how they might influence your steps today.

The Priest-King's Ministry of Rest

The next story, after Jesus's offer of restful work, is a very kinesthetic presentation. Jesus taught this lesson as He, His disciples, and some Pharisees walked through a field of unharvested grain.

> At that time Jesus went through the grain fields on the Sabbath, and His disciples became hungry and began to pick the heads of grain and eat. But when the Pharisees saw this, they said to Him, "Look, Your disciples do what is not lawful to do on a Sabbath." (Matthew 12:1–2)

The Pharisees had put many guidelines around how they thought the fourth commandment should be observed. They taught these rules to the people and then policed their enforcement. The Pharisees had determined that picking grain and eating it was a form of "harvesting," a type of work that they believed the sabbath commandment forbade.

Jesus then reminded them of a story from Scripture (1 Samuel 21) when David and his men showed up at the tabernacle and ate some bread that was there.

Have you not read what David did when he became hungry, he and his companions, how he entered the house of God, and they ate the consecrated bread, which was not lawful for him to eat nor for those with him, but for the priests alone? (Matthew 12:3–4)

The bread Jesus speaks of is the showbread in the tabernacle where, each week, twelve loaves of unleavened bread were placed on a table within the tabernacle. These loaves were replaced with new bread every sabbath. When the week-old bread was rotated out it was to be consumed only by the priests (Leviticus 24:6). This is the story Jesus chose to pull out of the history books for His lesson to the Pharisees.

At first, it might be difficult to figure out what Jesus is trying to say. Jesus and his disciples are out in a field picking grain. The Pharisees claim they are breaking the sabbath. Then Jesus says, don't you remember when David and his group of friends ate the priest's bread from the tabernacle?

On the surface this story just doesn't seem to fit the circumstances. I can only imagine what the Pharisees might have been thinking: "What? What does that story have to do with what's going on here?" But Jesus is a master teacher, and He's created a lesson for the Pharisees that includes parallel scenarios.

David Anointed . . . but Not Yet King

Let's remember the context of Jesus's Old Testament story about David. At that time, Saul was the acting king of Israel, even though God had removed His anointing. God's anointing was removed because Saul, the king, had acted like a priest and misused the tabernacle's ministry (1 Samuel 13:8–14).[66] God then instructed Samuel to anoint a mere boy, David, as the next king (1 Samuel 16:12–14). But Saul didn't leave office right away. In fact, Saul remained king of Israel for quite some time. When he learned that David had been identified as the next king, Saul attempted to retain his position of power by killing David. It was one of these times, when David was fleeing from Saul, that he went to the tabernacle and was given the showbread to eat.

This is the parallel scenario that Jesus recalls for the Pharisees. By doing so Jesus suggests that He, like David, had already been anointed ruler of God's kingdom (Matthew 3:13–17). But like Saul, the Pharisees, still in their position of power, no longer had God's anointing. The Pharisees had been pursuing Jesus to kill him in order to retain their position of power. Given this context, the story now seems to fit like a glove. Jesus masterfully picked this story and perfectly applied the parallel scenarios to condemn the Pharisees.

According to Dr. Carmen Joy Imes, "Surely Jesus had in mind the analogy to his own situation. The statement Jesus makes through the use of this story is subtle but radical. He seems to be suggesting that the same legal exemptions that applied in the case of David—Israel's true king in exile—also apply to him and his disciples."[67]

Let's consider some additional parallels between the two situations. Jesus then added, "Or have you not read in the Law, that on the Sabbath the priests in the temple break the Sabbath and are innocent?" (Matthew 12:5). Jesus reminded the Pharisees that those who work under God's rule and authority, the priests, do their work on the sabbath and are not guilty of breaking any of God's rules. When priests are in their place, doing their thing, God is pleased with their work. For priests, the sabbath is a day of work being yoked to God. That's what's supposed to happen on the sabbath.

Let me suggest that the same is true for believers today. Our restful existence is supposed to be filled with days of work being yoked to God. That may be a paradigm shift for most of you, but the New Testament often uses the "priestly" description for everyone that believes (1 Peter 2:5–9; Revelation 1:4–6; 5:6–10; 20:6).

Jesus suggests that He and His disciples, like priests, are doing their work on the sabbath and yet remain innocent. He then tells the Pharisees that the temple in Jerusalem is no longer the place to look for innocent priests doing God's work. To see those who are innocent, Jesus suggests, one need only look at Him and those attached to His yoke.

But I say to you that something greater than the temple is here. But if you had known what this means, "I desire compassion, and not a sacrifice," you would not have condemned the innocent. (Matthew 12:6–7)

Jesus claims to be the fulfillment of the temple ministry.[68] The temple's work takes place wherever Jesus and those yoked to Him are doing their work. No matter the day of the week, this is Jesus's picture of sabbath rest.

Lord of the Sabbath

What concluding statement does Jesus make for His lesson to the Pharisees? Well, it's another mic-drop moment for Jesus:

For the Son of Man is Lord of the Sabbath. (Matthew 12:8)

There it is . . . *bam!*

But let's make sure we hear Jesus clearly, and clarify what He is claiming in this statement. He is saying, "I am your rest. I am the Lord, and I hold the reins . . . *and* the reign of rest. I don't just make the rules, but I'm the Creator[69] of rest. It is only under My rule and authority that rest can occur. It is through attaching yourselves to Me and My ministry that you will find restful work, and that work can be done every day of the week. In fact, it should envelop your whole life."

Jesus is the only one that can bring functional rule, and good work, back to humanity. It is through trusting Him that each of us finds our purpose and our place. Apart from Him we continue working in the curse-a-day world, outside the garden-rule, and away from our rest.

Real-Life Parables

For Jesus to say that the Jubilee had been "fulfilled," that "something greater than the temple" had arrived, and that He was the "Lord of the Sabbath" is the same as saying God's rule has returned back to the creation. But people continue to be sick and die. So in at least one sense, while His rule is among us and offered to us, it hasn't yet fully been completed. Even though one stage of Christ's work is complete, there's still more work to be done. So, what does this mean for our present reality?

The story that follows Jesus's "Lord of the Sabbath" statement further illustrates what His rest truly is. In it, Jesus gives the Pharisees an unforgettable and practical visual lesson that demonstrates what His rest looks like.

In Matthew 12:9–15, departing from the grain fields where He had just been teaching, He entered a synagogue and healed a man's deformed hand:

> And a man was there whose hand was withered. And [the Pharisees] questioned Jesus asking, "Is it lawful to heal on the Sabbath?"—so that they might accuse Him. And He said to them, "What man is there among you who has a sheep, and if it falls into a pit on the Sabbath, will he not take hold of it and lift it out? How much more valuable then, is a man than a sheep! So then, it is lawful to do good on the Sabbath." (v. 10–12)

We have defined rest as a state when things are in their place and doing their thing. Jesus gives the Pharisees an example of a sheep in a pit. Everyone knows sheep are not supposed to be in pits. A sheep in a pit is not in its place to be . . . and it is not able to do what it is meant to do.[70]

In this story Jesus gives a physical picture of what it means for something to enter into rest and then He uses a man's hand to further illustrate His point.

Some of Jesus's stories, like this one, can be understood as real-life parables. Jesus's healing tells a story, in real life, that also portrays a spiritual truth. He heals the man's hand, but at the same time He attends to the man's spiritual condition. In that way, it's a parable.

Jesus took this opportunity, a sabbath day, to change a dysfunctional hand into a hand full of functional possibilities. He took the paralyzed[71] hand and restored it to its original purpose. Before Jesus, the hand didn't work correctly. After Jesus, it's able to do everything hands are supposed to do. Do you see Jesus undoing the results of the fall? He's pulling this man out of a pit on a seventh-day sabbath.

What was the Pharisees' response to this whole interchange? Well, they didn't have much to say, and they were infuriated by Jesus's lessons. In this sequence with the Pharisees Jesus had presented several lessons about rest, incorporating many learning styles, and yet the Pharisees proved to be students who were difficult to teach. Not only that, but they turned on the teacher.

> But the Pharisees went out and conspired against Him, as to how they might destroy Him. (Matthew 12:14)

Sometimes, no matter how creative the lesson plan—no matter how much time, energy, and thought one puts into the teaching process—some students are just not ready to learn![72] This was true even for Jesus.

But not everyone responded to Jesus like the Pharisees. His slow-clap ministry full of mic-drop moments was often received by others who were willing and ready to hear, watch, and learn. At the end of this Matthew passage, we are told that there were many that day who decided to yoke themselves to Jesus. As He withdrew from the Pharisees, many "followed him, and He healed them all" (Matthew 12:15). Those who followed Jesus that day experienced His ministry of restoration not just of their bodies, but more importantly their souls. It's this larger ministry, the restoration and healing of human souls, that Jesus offers each of us who decide to take advantage of His offer of rest.

> Take my yoke upon you . . . and you will find rest for your souls. (Matthew 11:29)

Signs of the New Covenant

In chapter 2, we discussed how God, in the Old Testament, often supplied signs for the covenants He instituted with humanity. We now recognize

God's sabbaths as the sign of the Mosaic covenant, and as described in this chapter, Jesus fulfilled each of those sabbaths. His ministry introduced an advanced understanding of rest, and simultaneously also unveiled a new covenant with humanity. You may be wondering, when Jesus fulfilled the Old and established the New, did He supply signs for this new covenant as well? Yes, He did! Jesus introduced one sign early in His ministry with John the Baptist at the Jordan River, and another with His disciples the night before His death.

As we discovered in our study, it's important for those involved in a covenant to understand which signs have been given and how they are to be implemented. To the extent that the covenant participants correctly display the signs, they become an effective signal to all of humanity illustrating what the covenant is all about. But to the extent the signs are not accurately presented, it can insert confusion about who God is, what He's already accomplished, and what the future holds for His covenantal partners. Regarding the new covenant, the signs convey the incredible method of salvation provided by Jesus's death, burial, and resurrection, and His ultimate plan to rule and subdue the entirety of creation.

The Sign of Baptism

When Jesus followed John the Baptist to the Jordan River, it was much more than a refreshing plunge in the Judean wilderness. In His baptism, Jesus dips into the symbolic waters of death and emerges alive to introduce a new covenant. It's the announcement of His plan to fulfill the ancient mission given to humanity to subdue and rule the earth, and baptism would become a sign of that covenant.

In the Gospels, John the Baptist introduced the start of something new by signaling the inefficiency of the old (Matthew 3:7–10). He then proclaimed that he was baptizing with water, but that One would come after him who would baptize with the Holy Spirit. Then, Jesus was baptized, the heavens opened, and the Spirit descended upon Him (Matthew 3:16). Water baptism is the outward sign of an inner covenantal initiation, and what happened in the Jordan River that day was an early introduction. But it's in the last words of Matthew's gospel where we find Jesus's instructions regarding the implementation of this sign.

> All authority has been given to Me in heaven and on earth. Go therefore and make disciples of all the nations, baptizing them in the name of the Father and the Son and the Holy Spirit, teaching them to observe all that I commanded you. (Matthew 28:18–20)

In several of his letters, Paul describes the spiritual baptism which takes place within a person's soul (Romans 6:1–14; 1 Corinthians 12:13; Galatians 3:26–29; Ephesians 4:4–6; Colossians 2:9–12). It's this inner transformation that becomes visible with the covenantal sign of water baptism. This baptism is an outward sign of what has already happened in the unseen initiation. A water baptism is how individuals openly display that they have joined Jesus's administration and mission to rule and subdue the new creation.

Unfortunately, in many modern settings, the covenantal sign of baptism is incorrectly represented. Baptism is often eclipsed by a prayer to "ask Jesus into your heart." But the modern use of the "sinner's prayer" has little, if any, biblical precedent. And where such prayers are presented as the first indication of salvation, the actual sign of covenant initiation, water baptism, is often relegated to a secondary role. It's common for believers, instilled with the confidence of a sinner's prayer, to postpone baptism for years, if not decades. In this way, modern evangelicalism has created a "new sign" for the new covenant. And at best, this substitution confuses the message and mission of Christ.

This was the case for both Lisa and me. We grew up in the same town but attended different churches, and we both became believers at a young age. When we expressed our early interest, we were directed to confirm our status by saying a sinner's prayer. Years later, I would learn that some ministries tally those prayers and determine the success of an event by the number of people that prayed them. As an adult, I've been involved in events where *the* pre-stated goal was a certain number of "decisions for Christ" that were tracked on a spreadsheet.

But for both Lisa and me, that initial prayer wasn't just a one-time event. Over the years, we were given multiple opportunities to repeat similar prayers, and I suspect we were counted again at every "Amen." At almost every event we attended (summer camps, weekend retreats, Easter-egg hunts, Christmas programs, and kids' choir) there was another opportunity to "accept Jesus into our hearts" through the use of another such invocation. But we knew we loved Jesus, and had never stopped believing in Him. For both of us, it was a confusing experience.

It was only years later, after we were married, that a sermon on baptism prompted us to reconsider our reality. We were leaders in our church, had outwardly professed our faith for years, and now were embarrassed by the prospect that we had never been physically baptized in water. So we both signed up and were baptized one Sunday morning in front of the entire congregation.

Our experience with baptism also greatly influenced how we chose to present it to our own children. When our boys Jake and Nate were young, they both expressed an early faith in Christ. And after several age-appropriate conversations about the nature of faith, and confirmation that that was what they were likely experiencing, Lisa and I encouraged them to consider baptism. The church we were attending, like many today, had a policy that baptism wasn't offered before a certain age, and our youngest son had not yet reached that boundary. So, I petitioned the pastor for an exception to the rule. I presented our process, and what I understood regarding the scriptural mandate for baptism, and He agreed to allow both of our boys to make their own decision. With this freedom, both Jake and Nate decided to take part in the initiation sign of the new covenant.

This is not to say that everything was entirely clear in the process. There were certainly areas of inconsistency. Both boys had said multiple prayers to accept Jesus into their hearts along the way, for they too had grown up in the church. I'll never forget the excited call we got from one church worker who, weeks after the boys' baptisms, called to tell us that one of them had prayed the sinner's prayer and accepted Jesus into his heart that day. And years later, when many of their friends were getting baptized, our sons wondered if they too should have waited. But most of our modern barriers and suggested delays surrounding baptism are not found within the Bible's description of the sign. So, when Lisa and I suspected they had truly experienced an inner renewal, we encouraged our sons to openly participate in the initiation sign of the new covenant.

Our choices also changed the perspective of others in our family. My grandparents had my dad baptized shortly after his birth. And as a young boy, he eventually came to believe in the mission and message of Christ. But since he was baptized as an infant, he wasn't sure if he should also be baptized as a sign of his initial faith experience. This theological question gnawed at him for decades. Much later in his life, my dad finally decided what he believed on the subject. And, on a trip to Israel with his entire family, he decided to resolve his dilemma. I had the privilege of baptizing my seventy-year-old father in the Jordan River, at the traditional site where Jesus experienced the same. Even though my dad waited many years to decide, his ultimate choice to participate in this covenantal sign was still a meaningful and very moving event.

When Jesus instituted the new covenant, He gave water baptism as the sign of our initiation. The biblical sequence is always for baptism to precede taking part in communion, but some modern practices commonly invert this arrangement. We have the opportunity, despite our present-day adaptations, to clarify His message and more correctly communicate His covenantal mission through the use of baptism. It is one way we acknowledge the Lord of the Sabbath as our leader.

The Sign of Communion

A second sign of the new covenant was instituted at Jesus's last meal with his disciples:

[T]he Lord Jesus in the night in which He was betrayed took bread; and when He had given thanks, He broke it and said, "This

is My body, which is for you; do this in remembrance of Me." In
the same way He took the cup also after supper, saying, "This cup
is the new covenant in My blood; do this, as often as you drink
it, in remembrance of Me." For as often as you eat this bread and
drink the cup, you proclaim the Lord's death until He comes. (1
Corinthians 11:23b–26)

When Jesus took the bread and the cup and served it, these two elements became symbols that stand for at least two things. The first might
be a little surprising, because we don't always associate it with communion. The author of Hebrews tells us that Jesus's death redeemed the
transgressions of the faithful who were a part of the old covenant:

For this reason, He is the mediator of a new covenant, so that,
since *a death has taken place for the redemption of the transgressions that were committed under the first covenant*, those who have
been called may receive the promise of the eternal inheritance.
(Hebrews 9:15, emphasis mine)

Let's remember, all those who attended the Last Supper had grown
up as participants in this old covenant, and Jesus was signaling the
redemption of the first through a process only He could accomplish. But
Jesus wasn't leaving them without a way. His redemption signaled the
fulfillment of the old, and at the same time it announced the beginning of
the new. Jesus was calling them out of the inefficiency of the one, so they
could receive the promise of the eternal in the second.

When He said, "A new covenant," He has made the first obsolete.
But whatever is becoming obsolete and growing old is ready to
disappear. (Hebrews 8:13)

Communion, then, is so much more than the nebulous reminder
of Jesus's death that we've made it in some of our modern practices. Its

significance is much wider than the tiny, stale wafer, and deeper than the watered-down thimble of juice, we often serve. I think we've forgotten, or maybe never even realized, the bread and the cup were originally attached to a meaningful and fully satisfying fellowship meal.

Communion is a symbol for what Jesus's death accomplished, in the liminal time, between two covenants. It signals the seemingly impossible redemption of the sin of the one, and the incredible putting away of the sin of the other (Hebrews 9:26).

When Jesus served the cup He said, "this is the new covenant in My blood."

I'm not sure if you've thought about those words in the context of the establishment of the new covenant. Those who take communion are acknowledging they have, through faith, entered into a covenant with God. A covenant is a spiritual agreement, but what exactly does this mean in the context of communion?

There's a scene in the Old Testament, in Exodus 24, that I believe fore-shadows our New Testament practice of communion. When Moses received the old covenant from God on Mt. Sinai, the text says that he collected the blood of some sacrificed animals in basins. He then took the book of the covenant and read it in the hearing of the people; and they said, "All that the LORD has spoken we will do, and we will be obedient!" (v. 7). Each person said this individually, but they also said it collectively as a community.

Then Moses did something that seems really weird . . . and maybe a little gross as well! Moses took the blood from the basins, sprinkled it on the people, and said, "Behold the blood of the covenant, which the LORD has made with you in accordance with all these words" (v. 8).

"The blood of the covenant . . ." That should sound familiar to our New Testament ears. It's the way Jesus introduced the cup at the Last Supper.

At Mt. Sinai, the people heard and understood the law, promised to follow it, and then the blood was sprinkled on them. This was how the old covenant was ratified, but the old covenant was written on stone tablets. The covenant that Jesus offers is far better (Hebrews 9:18–26).

The details of the new covenant are described in the Scriptures, but the implementation of that law is written on the pliable hearts of believers, not the rigid rocks of Sinai (2 Corinthians 3:1–8; Hebrews 8:7–13). When we come to faith in Christ, we agree to follow the covenant that was spoken by Jesus and is being written on each of our hearts by the work of the Holy Spirit.

So, when believers participate in communion, it's as if we say, similarly to those ancient Israelites, "All that the Scriptures have explained regarding the new covenant, and everything the Holy Spirit will communicate along our path, we agree . . . and we will do."

I'm not sure if you noticed one significant difference in this ceremony: Jesus doesn't sprinkle us, like Moses did on the exterior, with the blood of the new covenant. Rather, He invites us to *drink* it! We internalize it as a symbol of the cleansing power that it has on our innermost being. We ingest it because that is where it symbolically does its work—on our souls.

Communion is a time to remember the death of Christ who redeemed us from the imperfection of the old. And it's also a sign to remind us, individually and as a covenant community, that we have agreed to follow the Holy Spirit's direction as a part of the new. And this is the very voice that will lead us to the new covenant fulfillment of sabbath rest that Christ offers.

God has established covenantal signs as visible indicators of His work in the world. The signs of the Mosaic covenant, God's sabbaths, have all been fulfilled by Jesus through His ministry of rest. His offer of rest is more efficient and effective than the shadowy reminders of the first covenant. And the signs He's given for the new covenant more effectively display the rest He offers. Baptism is the initial sign Christ gave for a believer's entrance into the covenant, and communion is a repetitive sign of our ongoing involvement.

To the extent that we have changed the order, added to, misrepresented, or incorrectly applied any of these signs, it presents a great opportunity for correction and clarification. We can reestablish water baptism as the sign it was intended to be. It represents the initial dying to our will, reception of the Holy Spirit, and alignment under the restful rule of Christ. We also have the occasion to reframe biblical rest when we participate in communion. The bread and the cup constitute a meaningful fellowship meal that can reflect the rest that Christ offers.

These signs are an opportunity to publicly display Christ's fulfillment of the old, and His inauguration of something new. So let's follow the Lord of the Sabbath into the rest that He offers and display that truth, as best we can, within His creation.

ADDITIONAL REST RESOURCES

CHAPTER 5

THERE REMAINS A SABBATH REST

One hand full of rest is better than two fists full of labor and striving after wind.

—Ecclesiastes 4:6

In the previous chapters, we've unpacked much about how God interacts with rest. We've seen what rest was in the beginning, considered the use of reminders after the exile, and examined how Jesus presented Himself as the fulfillment of the idea during His earthly ministry. To revisit the "neighborhood" analogy from earlier, we've ventured into the complex system of streets in the neighborhood of rest without getting stuck at the bottom of the bag. But we are not done exploring the neighborhood. We still need to ask possibly the most practical questions of the entire journey:

So what?

We know what biblical rest is—so what now?

It's in the "so what" question that we will unpack how biblical rest is supposed to make sense in our day-to-day lives. We will think through how believers can interact with this topic. We will locate specific examples of how to enter that rest, and how to remain there.

It's in Hebrews that the application will become much more practical. We will see how the ministry of Jesus is compared and contrasted with the shadow ministry of the Old Testament Law. In its case for Jesus, Hebrews continually finds the Law lacking in its ability to fix what is wrong, and presents Jesus as fully sufficient in those regards. It's also in Hebrews (chapters 3 and 4) that we find the most in-depth discussion on the topic of rest in the entirety of the New Testament. It is there that many of the practical "so what?" questions of rest are answered.

To better understand that discussion in Hebrews 3–4, let's begin by venturing down a side street of the neighborhood and look at a conclusion that the author of Hebrews makes regarding the Law in Hebrews 10. We've previously looked at the first verse of that chapter, which speaks of the Law as a shadow ministry. But that first verse is a small part of a much bigger discussion (Hebrews 10:1–14) in which the sacrificial system is contrasted with Jesus. Let's look at that first verse again:

> For the Law, since it has only a shadow of the good things to come and not the very form of things, can never, by the same sacrifices which they offer continually year by year, make perfect those who draw near. (Hebrews 10:1)

Sometimes people get thrown off when it says "perfect" at the end. What does it even mean for a person to be "made perfect"? How would someone even track that? The Greek word behind the translation can also carry the sense of completeness, fulfillment, or maybe best in this context, maturity. It has a much deeper meaning than our English translations can easily convey. I like the idea that as something matures, it approaches the fulfillment or completeness of what it is supposed to be. This is very good news as we all grow older. Those around me have been waiting for so long for my maturity to take root!

This passage suggests the Old Testament sacrifices, the shadows, are incapable of bringing people to maturity. It says there is no way the shadows can bring someone to their fulfillment or the completeness of what they are supposed to be. The logic backing this statement is found in the next two verses.

> Otherwise, would they not have ceased to be offered, because the worshipers, having once been cleansed, would no longer have had consciousness of sins? But in those sacrifices, there is a reminder of sins year by year. (Hebrews 10:2–3)

This is the reason these sacrifices are incapable of getting humanity to the finish line, the ultimate goal of completeness and maturity. It's the repetition of their application that proves their overall inefficiency. It's a red flag to let us know that they were incapable of bringing people to the end goal.

It's in these repetitive sacrifices that there is a reminder of sins, year by year. Did you hear that? The way that is worded should have grabbed your attention. We've spent a significant amount of time discussing the idea of the Law containing reminders. That's one of the main purposes of the Law: to remind people that there is a God who created this whole thing and that He has a plan to fix it. The Old Testament sacrifices were a reminder of that, but it wasn't only the sacrifices. The whole Law was a comprehensive, well-coordinated, interconnected system of reminders.

What was the end goal of the Old Testament Law? The goal was for Israel to live in a relationship with God, where they were in their place and doing the thing they were created to do without sin or a lack of faith, hindering God's kingdom work. That was the goal, but Hebrews argues that the Law was incapable of accomplishing that goal. Humanity needed something better that could complete the task.

It is the new covenant of Jesus's ministry that fully unshackles humanity. This unhindered existence will be fully realized at the end of the story (Revelation 21–22). But the author of Hebrews talks about the ministry of Jesus being available to humanity now, not just at some point in the seemingly far-distant future. That's an important distinction that many people overlook in the argument. The realization of our "maturity" is not just an end goal to which we can only look forward. Through the ministry of Jesus, humanity is able to begin the maturation process now.

So, in contrast to the continual and repetitive sacrifices that were only shadows of something better to come, the body of Jesus was offered one time for all people and all time (Hebrews 10:10). Jesus is the answer to the shadowy sacrifices. It's through His one offering that the end goal is available. It's through Jesus, because he is better than the old shadows, that humanity can be brought to its maturity. We can be made whole. This was the ultimate end goal of the Eden experience. The garden was to expand, fill the earth, and bring God's rule over the whole of creation.

Wells and Springs

Much of this discussion (Jesus vs. the Law) can seem rather abstract to modern readers. We are so distant from the original context of Israel and the ancient Near East that we sometimes just can't relate. I've spent the last few days trying to think of a more modern illustration, and now I'd like to share it.

I've mentioned before that Lisa and I currently live on a small piece of property just a few miles from our town. We've come to realize that living on small acreage has multiple benefits, but it also comes with a few unique responsibilities. Water is one of them.

Our property does not have access to many of the normal city utilities. We get electricity . . . but that's about it. There's no natural gas, city water, or city sewer offered to people who live on our street. But maybe most importantly, at least according to our two sons, there are no great options for obtaining high-speed internet! For years our access to the world was through a satellite connection that wasn't very good when it rained. Did I mention we live in Oregon? Unfortunately, it rains quite a bit.

When we built our house, we made plans for these deficiencies. For instance, we use electricity instead of natural gas to heat the home and cook our meals. We installed a septic tank with a drain field to compensate for the lack of a city sewer connection. We also installed a well on our property as the water source.

The well works great. It's connected to a pump and a pressure tank that supplies good clean water to the entire property. The only problem is when the electricity goes out. This usually happens once or twice a year for short periods of time. When that happens, everything shuts down and no water comes out of the faucets. Power outages remind me that the water isn't just naturally flowing. It takes energy, effort, and money to get that water to flow.

It used to be, years ago, that properties like mine came standard with a hand pump or a bucket to get water out of a well. Every day, people would go to the well to get enough water to supply the household's needs. A well or cistern is a man-made way of providing water. Getting water from that source is repetitive, and it requires effort and maintenance. A well will never just supply clean water on its own.

But some properties contain natural springs which replace the need to manually retrieve water. With a spring, water flows up and out of the ground and continually cleanses itself. Springs are superior to wells because they continuously produce life-giving water.

In many ways, the Old Testament Law is like a well with a bucket. It requires humanity to visit repetitively, over and over again, to access water and quench thirst. In contrast to the well, Jesus's ministry is like a natural spring where the life-giving water continually flows and satisfies humanity's thirst once and for all. This analogy might sound familiar because it's the basis of a conversation Jesus had with a Samaritan woman (John 4:7–30). Jesus was resting at a well originally dug by Jacob, the father of the nation of Israel. Jesus used that well as an analogy for the Old Testament Law:

Everyone who drinks of this water will thirst again; but whoever drinks of the water that I will give him shall never thirst; but the water that I will give him will become in him a well of water springing up to eternal life. (John 4:14)

Later in the conversation, Jesus explains the analogy:

Woman, believe Me, an hour is coming when neither in this mountain nor in Jerusalem will you worship the Father . . . but an hour is coming, and now is, when the true worshipers will worship the Father in spirit and truth. (John 4:21, 23)

The well water from Jesus's analogy symbolizes the imperfect repetitive worship practices of the Law. Jesus was announcing the fulfillment of the well—a natural cleansing spring that will cleanse and quench thirst from within.

Here's maybe the most important point of the whole story: Jesus said that the use of the well was already becoming obsolete, and that the living water was available for the taking. The ministry of Jesus's living water was fully available way back then for the Samaritan woman. If that was true then, it's also fully available today for the true worshipers of God.

He Takes Away the First . . .

This concept of "once-for-all sufficiency" is presented in Hebrews 10:10, specifically regarding the sacrifices. But let's back up just one verse and look further at the description the author gives.

He said, "Behold, I have come to do Your will." He takes away the first in order to establish the second. (Hebrews 10:9)

Who is the "He" in this verse? In this context, who is it that takes away the sacrificial system and offers His own body in its place? It's Jesus himself.

This is totally understandable when we talk about sacrifices. Most people today would, hopefully, agree that we no longer have to sacrifice animals at an altar to experience forgiveness, but the conversation often gets stuck when considering what to do with the other parts of the Old Testament Law. We know Christ's sacrifice fulfills the animal sacrifices, but what other types of "once-for-all sufficiency" does Jesus bring to the other parts of the Law?

The author of Hebrews presents one all-encompassing argument about how Jesus is the fulfillment of the entire Mosaic Law. From the beginning to the end of the book, Jesus is found to be fully sufficient. There's never a point in the argument where the author pauses to suggest, "This part, or that part, of the Mosaic Law isn't fulfilled by Jesus; therefore believers should still observe that part of the shadow ministry."

It's important to understand this larger context as we travel back to the discussion in Hebrews 3–4 of sabbatical rest. If the "overall sufficiency of Jesus's ministry" is true, we should expect to see the same theological approach being used there in relation to the seventh-day sabbath.

Jesus is the one who takes away the first. What is he taking away? In Hebrews 10 it's the shadowy repetitive sacrifices in the law. They were repeatedly observed and yet they could never bring people completeness or maturity in regard to the fight against sin. Why did those aspects of the Law need to be removed? Jesus took the repetitive shadow ministry away because, if left in place, it would cause people to focus on the shadows when in reality the Substance had arrived. He knew the well would distract humanity's attention away from the source of natural spring water. So He "takes away the first," not just because He feels like it but because the taking away has a purpose. It allows people to focus on the fulfillment, the only thing that can get humanity to the end goal of maturity.

Humanity needed the imperfect reminders (before Jesus came) to know that this isn't the way it's supposed to be. They were reminders of our problem, and they were sufficient for their time. But ultimately the shadows can get in the way of clearly understanding the Substance. It is this conclusion, regarding sacrifices, that will help us in our application of rest. So now, let's take our conversation back to Hebrews 3–4.

It's Back to Work . . .

> For if Joshua had given them rest, He would not have spoken of another day after that. (Hebrews 4:8)

The author of Hebrews uses similar logic regarding the repetitive shadow ministry of rest. The reminders of rest in the Old Testament were not one-time events. As we have seen, they were very repetitive. They happened once a week, as well as several other times a year attached to the festivals, every seventh sabbatical year, and every fiftieth jubilee year. Eventually these repetitions were applied in a land of rest where the people were reminded on a daily basis of God's faithfulness.

As we apply the logic of John 4 and Hebrews 10 to this discussion, what does the repetition of the reminders of rest suggest? What does it suggest they are incapable of? They are not able to get humanity to the final destination, the end goal of completeness, maturity, and our fulfillment as people. In actuality—and rather ironically too—it's in these shadows of sabbath that we are reminded of our *unrest*. They are a reminder of humanity's sin.

This played out each week not only in taking a day off from the work of the curse, but in knowing each week that Saturday night was coming. In the Israelite community, when Saturday night at sunset arrived, it was time to get back to the work of the curse-a-day world. In modernity, we might think of this as "Monday's a coming." And what's the general attitude behind that idea? "Ugh . . . I've got to go back to work! I can't believe the weekend is already gone."

By taking time off and resting from working in a cursed land, humanity is reminded that we are living the majority of our lives in unrest. But if these shadows of rest were able to bring about maturity and fulfillment, if they were able to get us to true rest, they would not have been repetitive in nature . . . just like the sacrifices.

So, if Joshua had given them rest, He would not have spoken of another day after that. Who is the "He" here? I'm going to suggest something a little different. It's not David (the author of the psalm being quoted). And I don't think it's God the Father either. In the context of Hebrews, the focus is always Jesus. It's Jesus who speaks of a new day regarding rest. It's Jesus who takes away the first in order to establish the second.

> For if Joshua had given them rest, He [Jesus] would not have spoken of another day after that. So there remains a Sabbath rest for the people of God. (Hebrews 4:8–9)

The next question to ask is, "What is it regarding sabbath rest that remains?"

The answer to that question is, "Whatever type of rest Jesus offers . . . *that's* what remains."

I'll agree that it's easy, and sometimes inviting, to go back to the repetition of the shadows. But they can easily become "checklist items" which are marked off at regular intervals, and then forgotten again until the next time they appear on the list. Could it be that participating in a shadow ministry of repetitive rest might distract from what Jesus now offers? As we walk through the remainder of this study, I invite you to contemplate with me what type of rest Jesus has brought to the table. Is it only one day a week that He allows us to experience rest, or is the fulfillment of rest something that is available every day of every week on the calendar?

Let me frame this a little more dramatically by purposely *misquoting* some of Jesus's words. When Jesus offers His rest to the weary (Matthew 11:28), do you suppose what He really meant to say was, "Come to me, all of you folks who are spiritually tired, and I will give you . . . respite care one day a week"?

We instinctually know that Jesus's offer is so much more than a lazy Sunday. And yet, historically, that's where many have landed. Since Jesus is offering the fulfillment of rest, let's further consider what that means.

Ironic Joshua

The Greek word Ἰησοῦς (pronounced "Ee-ay Seuss!") is translated into English as two different names, "Joshua" and "Jesus." Translators have done this for reasons of clarity. Let me explain.

When translators think the New Testament text is referencing Joshua, the one who succeeded Moses in the Old Testament, they translate Ἰησοῦς into English as "Joshua" (Acts 7:45; Hebrews 4:8). But when they suspect the New Testament text is referring to the New Testament character, the one who healed people and walked on water, they translate Ἰησοῦς as "Jesus." The latter is by far the most common and happens 902 times in the New Testament.[73]

But make no mistake, in the Greek "Jesus" and "Joshua" are the same name. It's important to understand, from a Jewish perspective, that Joseph and Mary were instructed to name their son Joshua. It was a name loaded with meaning, historical context, and cultural significance.

In Hebrews 4:8 the correct referent for Ἰησοῦς is the Joshua character who succeeded Moses: "For if *Joshua* had given them rest . . ." But interestingly, some of the very early English translations picked the wrong referent in their translation. To this day the King James Version still reads, "For if *Jesus* had given them rest, then would he not afterward have spoken of another day."

But that mistranslation completely changes the message that Hebrews is attempting to convey. If, as according to the King James Version, it is *Jesus* who is unable to offer the ultimate rest, everything is turned upside down. Thankfully all of the modern English translations, including The New King James Version, have caught that early error and correctly state the referent, in Hebrews 4:8, as "Joshua" instead of "Jesus."

What I don't want you to miss is the linguistic irony happening in the passage. It's an irony the author of Hebrews expected his readers to see. He mentions Joshua as the character that brings the Old Testament community into the shadow of the Promised Land, but that process didn't work. That wasn't true rest.

He would not have spoken of another day after that. (Hebrews 4:8b)

The "He" here is a general reference to God, and I've already suggested that in the context of Hebrews we could easily say it's Jesus. But let's not even read it that way. I'm going to change it up yet again. Let's read it as "Joshua," because that's the way the original readers would have understood Jesus's name.

What's the irony? This verse could be understood as saying the following:

For if [the Old Testament] Joshua had given them rest, He [the New Testament Joshua] would not have spoken of another day after that. (Hebrews 4:8)

Jesus is the new Joshua. He is a Joshua who is better than the Old Testament character because He brings a better ministry. He brings humanity into a better place of rest. He does not do this in a shadow world, but in reality. That's the ironic twist hidden within this statement about rest.

Biblical Codependency

Now we begin a more in-depth look at another aspect of Hebrews 3–4. This is where we will specifically be looking for the answer to the "so what" question. We will see that these chapters in Hebrews have a codependent relationship with some passages in the Old Testament.

My wife Lisa is a counselor. She's really good at what she does and has been fortunate to help many individuals and couples through life's sticky situations. I've also been the beneficiary of her professional expertise. When she was in school for her master's in counseling, she became more familiar with the dangers of "codependent relationships." What's a codependent relationship? Well, in the counseling world, it's an excessive emotional or psychological reliance one might have with a partner. It's unhealthy and can stunt personal growth and natural independence. Soon after learning about this, my wife and I quickly recognized we were involved in an unhealthy codependent relationship.

Hi, my name is Greg, my partner is "coffee in the morning" and I am codependent!

Whereas codependency is not good in personal relationships, Bible passages are often written to be codependent upon each other, and that's a good thing. It means that if we are to fully understand one passage, we must also understand the "excessive reliance" it has on its partner passages. The New Testament authors often wrote in this codependent way, matching a New Testament concept with its Old Testament partners. When this type of codependency was the author's original intent, we readers do a disservice to the text when we don't understand the dynamics of the whole relationship.

This is exactly what we find in Hebrews 3–4. The Hebrews passage is codependent upon portions of Psalm 95. And we will find that Psalm 95 is codependent on a story from Exodus 17. That's a codependent relationship involving three partners! My wife tells me this type of situation can get very complicated, so let me try and counsel you through it. Let's stop for a moment, get a Bible out, take a deep breath, and walk slowly through these passages. Like Lisa says, it's complicated.

Let's start by looking at the passage in Hebrews 3:7–11 that quotes part of Psalm 95 (I've italicized the codependent quote of Psalm 95 for clarity):

Therefore, just as the Holy Spirit says, "Today if you hear his voice, do not harden your hearts as when they provoked me, as in the day of trial in the wilderness, where your fathers tried me by testing me and saw my works for forty years. Therefore, I was angry with this generation, and said, 'They always go astray in their heart, and they did not know my ways'; as I swore in my wrath, 'They shall not enter my rest.'"

This portion of Hebrews quotes Psalm 95:7–11, which discusses the generation of Old Testament people who followed Moses out of Egypt. But this isn't the only time the author of Hebrews interacts with that particular psalm. We see it pop up again in Hebrews 3:15; and 4:3, 5, 7. For some reason the author has created a codependency between the discussion of rest in Hebrews 3–4 with this part of Psalm 95. To more fully understand biblical rest, the author of Hebrews sees it as necessary to take us back to that particular psalm.

If you place the Hebrews passage right next to the psalm for comparison, you may notice that there are differences between how the psalm is written in the Old Testament and the way it is quoted in Hebrews. Theologians spend a lot of time examining these types of translational differences. One of those scholars, Dr. Karen H. Jobes,[74] explains:

> [T]he Old Testament used by the Greek-speaking people of the first century was a Greek translation of the Hebrew Bible that is known as the Septuagint. . . . This is why sometimes in our English Bible a quotation of the Old Testament in the New actually might not match the corresponding Old Testament verse when we flip back to it. The New Testament writer is quoting an ancient Greek translation of the Old Testament, and our English Old Testament is translated from the Hebrew. There is a whole field of study called Septuagint studies that examines and debates why the ancient Greek translation appears somewhat different in places from the Hebrew Scriptures we know today.[75]

We won't focus on most of the irregularities found in Hebrews 3–4,[76] except to pay attention to two place names: Meribah and Massah (Psalm 95:8). Hebrews 3:8 translates the meaning of those names (shown here in italics): "do not harden your hearts as when *they provoked me* [Meribah], as in the *day of trial* [Massah] in the wilderness."

By tracking the Hebrews quote back to Psalm 95, we discover that the "rebellion" being discussed isn't describing the people's behavior during the entire time they were in the wilderness. Rather, the psalm refers to the specific rebellious events that happened at Meribah and Massah.

This might cause you to wonder, "Well then, what exactly happened at Meribah and Massah?" And that's a great question! It's the question the author of Hebrews wants you to ask, and it shows you're beginning to understand the codependency of these passages. A quick check of cross-references[77] reveals that the two place names are associated with a story back in Exodus 17:1–7.

The author of Hebrews codependently uses Psalm 95, then Psalm 95 brings Exodus 17:1–7 into the relationship, and that's where things get complicated.

Codependency Chart

Well, that escalated quickly![78] So let's consider this chart, which describes what we've just discovered:

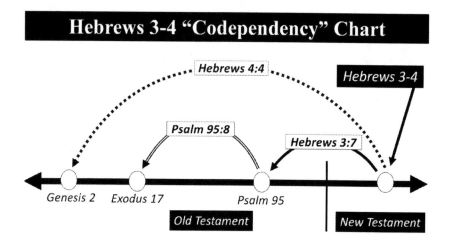

First let's locate Hebrews 3–4 within the New Testament (on the right side). We just noticed that Hebrews 3:7 sends us back to Psalm 95 (the solid line arch). And the mention of Meribah and Massah in Psalm 95:8 sends us back to Exodus 17 (the double line arch). Lastly, back in chapter one of this book, we tracked Hebrews 4:4 back to God's rest on the seventh day of creation in Genesis 2 (the dashed line arch on top).

When the author of Hebrews talks about rest, the idea is described in terms of these Old Testament passages. The original readers would have understood these examples intuitively, because the Old Testament was their history. Modern readers are often not as familiar with Old Testament stories . . . so we need a chart. And that's OK.

In a counseling session, realizing that a codependency exists is only the first step in solving the problem. Now let's figure out what all these relationships mean. Something that happened in Exodus 17 (at Meribah and Massah) has a direct relationship with the type of rest being described in the book of Hebrews. The author of Hebrews is warning us to not harden our hearts like the people did in that story, because they missed out on their opportunity of rest.

I've had the opportunity to do a little bit of traveling. Lisa and I have enjoyed several trips in the car to places close to where we live, but we've also had the opportunity to fly to places far away. I've found that travel always seems like a bit of a task. There's the packing, the planning, and the preparing that always ends up being more work than I think it will be. Probably the most complicated trips I've taken are when I've traveled with groups to Israel. For these trips I usually host three or four pre-trip meetings to discuss things we will encounter on the journey. I make suggestions about what to pack, what type of power converters are needed in that part of the world, how much cash to take, and when to apply for a passport. Those trips are much more complicated than a simple road trip with the family.

You might be starting to feel as if this Hebrews passage is taking us on a bit of a complicated journey. To be sure, a trip like this, which requires us to venture into the ancient Near Eastern culture and pop into and out of several different time periods, is not an easy trip. Rest is a complicated topic, but the journey is worth it. So let's continue exploring this elaborate neighborhood of rest.

In the next chapter we will dig a little deeper into these Old Testament stories and find some real "boots on the ground"—practical steps of how to enter godly rest. There's a rest that remains after the shadows have been taken away. It's a rest that will allow you to thrive and be exactly who you were created to be. You'll really like the destination, so let's continue on our journey.

ADDITIONAL

REST

RESOURCES

CHAPTER 6

A TRIFECTA OF TESTS

I've recently had the opportunity to teach Bible survey courses at a few universities near where I live. A survey course is just meant to be a quick overview of the Bible. The classes are generally twelve to fifteen weeks long, and each class usually covers the content of either the Old Testament or the New Testament. As you can imagine, with that amount of content and that number of weeks, there's only enough time to discuss a limited number of biblical stories and themes. Covering the content of one testament of the Bible is one thing, but in one of my classes, I had fifteen weeks to cover both the Old and New Testaments. The whole Bible! The tempo of *that* class was exceedingly fast and furious. It gave new meaning to the term "overview."

While I always enjoy the opportunity in these classes to discuss major themes (like biblical rest) from a broad perspective, sometimes the rapid pace of the class can be frustrating for both teacher and student. Many in my classes have grown up in families where Bible stories were regularly read, but for some, my classes are their very first exposure to the biblical content. This presents a great opportunity for me, but also a bit of a dilemma when it comes to grading. I continually try to think of ways to adequately assess each student's grasp of the content. I want it to be challenging for those with a lot of Bible background, while not overwhelming for those who are hearing the content for the first time. How have I solved this problem?

Three tests. A trifecta of tests. That's where I've landed.

In my classes I give three tests, but not all the tests are of equal weight. The first two tests are worth a lower percentage of the overall grade. The last one, the final, is worth more. Why do I set it up this way? Well, I've found that it takes a while for students to get to know me, my teaching style, and the types of questions I like to write. After the first test, we take time in class to go over all the questions and answers. Those who perform poorly the first time usually do better on the second exam, simply because they know their teacher better. By the time we get to the final, everyone knows exactly what to expect. They know what style of questions they will see; they have the class notes available; and if they've done their homework, everyone can pass that test. In fact, I usually start the first day of class by reassuring all the students. I tell them, "The gospel is good news, and today the gospel is that everyone can pass this class!"

But unfortunately, as with most classes, not everyone does.

We could imagine God's relationship with the Hebrew people as this type of teacher/student relationship. As we read through the stories at the beginning of Exodus, we can think of it as God, the teacher, allowing His students to become familiar with who He is, how he operates his class, and what type of tests will be given. God introduces Himself, walks His students through the class syllabus,[79] then takes everyone on a field trip out of slavery to the shores of the Red Sea.

Interestingly, right after passing through the Red Sea (in Exodus 14), there is a series of three "tests" (that's actually what they are called in the text). It's a test trifecta, and just like in my classes, the final test is worth more than the first two. These three tests will explain why that wilderness generation failed to pass their class . . . and enter their rest.

In fact, these tests are a key to understanding the puzzle of biblical rest from Hebrews 3–4. Why would I say that? Because the last of these tests was administered at a place called Meribah and Massah! That's not a description of two different places; it's just one location where something went so horribly wrong that it got two names. It's where the people failed their final exam.

Now, let's zoom in, and look at the series of events in Exodus 14–17 a little more closely.

They Cried Out to the Lord

In Exodus 14, after the people had left Egypt, they found themselves on the shore of the Red Sea with Pharaoh chasing them. They were in a seemingly impossible situation, one they couldn't solve by themselves.

> As Pharaoh drew near, the sons of Israel looked, and behold, the Egyptians were marching after them, and they became very frightened; so, the sons of Israel cried out to the LORD. Then they said to Moses, "Is it because there were no graves in Egypt that you have taken us away to die in the wilderness? Why have you dealt with us in this way, bringing us out of Egypt?" (Exodus 14:10–11)

You might be tempted to focus in on the end of that conversation with Moses, but did you notice what they did first? They cried out to the Lord. I think that's a good thing. Crying out to the Lord is often a desperate plea for help. It is what humanity tends to do when they can't solve something by themselves. It's how people cope when they think there might be a God who can help them get through their circumstances. I think this first response is a good one, but then it's hard to ignore what immediately followed.

Then they said to Moses, "Grumble . . . grumble . . . complain . . . complain."

The people immediately began complaining about their circumstances. Later in the story of the exodus, these same people further develop this habit of grumbling and complaining, and interestingly, we won't hear them cry out to the Lord very often. Moses will cry out on their behalf, but we just don't see the people doing it much.

Let's pause here and ask a few questions. What exactly is grumbling and complaining? Well, for the Israelites in the desert, their complaining usually took the form of questioning God's plan for their lives and for their redemption. Grumbling was their way of saying they knew a better way to run things than God. Does that sound familiar at all?

It should, because that's exactly how Adam and Eve responded in the garden of Eden. Their story doesn't say they grumbled and complained—it just says they chose to eat a piece of fruit from a tree—but the core of these two responses is the same. Both responses question the function and order that God has prepared and suppose there's a better way.

Did the Hebrews have a better plan? Well, they thought they did. They figured it would have been better to have remained in slavery in Egypt. *That* was their plan . . . to go back into slavery.

But, that's a horrible plan!

This seems rather obvious to us as we read the story, but remember, we have *their* entire story at our disposal. We have the benefit of knowing where God was trying to take them and we know how much their existence in slavery paled in comparison to that of the Promised Land.

The Israelites were making decisions without the benefit of everything we know. Egypt was all they knew, and it was strangely comfortable—so comfortable in fact, that they longed to go back to slavery even while poised right on the cusp of freedom. I think this is a human condition. Sometimes people choose to return to horrible circumstances even when an escape route is available. Change, even change for the better, is often very uncomfortable and scary.

Now let's ask, how might your story be similar? How might we apply these lessons to our own circumstances? Odds are that you've been caught in some sort of slavery to something. In Romans 6, Paul presents humanity's relationship to sin as a type of slavery, and in *our* journey out of sin, God often leads us through situations we can't solve on our own.

Has this been your experience? When was the last time life pinned you down against the shores with no way to escape? Was it a financial situation? Was it something seemingly impossible at work? Was it an internal struggle, or something to do with your family?

Maybe more important than the type of situation you faced is this next question: Do you remember how you responded? Did you expectantly cry out to the Lord when faced with what was impossible without Him? If you did, what came out of your mouth next?

Was it "Grumble . . . grumble?" Did you "Complain . . . complain?"

It's easy to complain when we can't yet see the end of *our* story. But let's agree to recognize this type of response for what it is. Through our grumbling we communicate to God our lack of confidence in His function and order for the world. It's how we suggest we could have done better. It confirms that we are like the Hebrew people in the wilderness. But maybe more importantly, it solidifies our ancestry all the way back to Adam and Eve.

The author of the book of Hebrews is correct! *Our* story *is* similar to the wilderness generation and our trip out of slavery will also lead us into seemingly impossible situations. These crisis points give us the opportunity to make decisions that can either lead to rest or further wandering.[80] They are opportunities to either grumble and complain, or to trust the teacher's faithfulness.

Now, let's see how Moses responded to the people's grumbling.

Just Pick Your Seat for the Show

> But Moses said to the people, "Do not fear! Stand by and see the salvation of the Lord which He will accomplish for you today. . . . The Lord will fight for you while you keep silent." (Exodus 14:13–14)

Did you notice Moses's first instruction?

Do not fear!

That's interesting . . . and instructive. If there really is a God, you don't have to fear situations you can't solve on your own. I feel like I could just stop right here for a while and work on that. Maybe you could too. If God really is the one who brought functional order to the cosmos, and if He is the one who knows why things were created and how everything works, then seemingly impossible situations give us an opportunity to trust Him. There's no need to try and create our own system of function and order. We don't have to fear when we lack solutions.

Then Moses says, "Stand by . . ."

He's not instructing the people to just move aside. Maybe a better way to say this is "Get to a place where you can see what's about to happen, because you don't want to miss this." He's telling them to pick their seat for the show. God's about to do something big!

When God works, His nature is revealed. When that happens, it's important to be in a position—physically, emotionally, psychologically, and spiritually—to recognize His work. It's one of the fastest ways for students to get to know their teacher. So take a stand and see the salvation of the Lord, which He will accomplish for you today.

Then Moses says, "The LORD will fight for you while you keep silent." The Hebrew word for "keep silent" is used almost fifty times in the Old Testament. The word has a lot of different senses to it. But most often it means just what it sounds like it means.

Shut up!

Just . . . stop . . . talking!

Or in this context, maybe: stop grumbling and complaining!

But in some other contexts, the word is translated as "listen in silence." Slow down, listen to the silence, and hear from the Lord.[81] It can also refer to someone who is deaf, someone who is unable to hear. Used in this sense, it could mean, "The Lord will fight for you, even when you are unable to hear."

It's almost as if Moses is saying, "The Lord will fight for you while you, you who are deaf . . . while you stop your speaking . . . while you listen in silence. Just take your silent stand and, from that perspective, see the salvation He will accomplish for you."

When we're not complaining, and we find ourselves in silence with the Lord, then we're in a position where we can listen. Listen for what? Well, for whatever it is that God wants to communicate. And God can communicate any number of different ways. In this specific story, God communicated by parting the waters.

This whole message ties nicely back into the instructions in Psalm 95:7: "Today, if you would hear his voice . . .".

Did you notice the "if" there? The psalmist didn't say "*when* you hear His voice." He said, "*if* you would hear," which lends to the option of not hearing. There is a possibility that you won't hear. How is that likely to happen? Well, if we are complaining too much, we might miss it. If we are not listening, we might miss it. If we've gotten to a point in our lives where, spiritually speaking, we've become deaf, we might just miss it.

Let's Get a Move On

Then the LORD said to Moses, "Why are you crying out to Me? Tell the sons of Israel to go forward." (Exodus 14:15)

God says, "Let's get a move on!" This suggests that people can be "listening" for God's voice and still be "active" and "going forward." We might be tempted to think that the only time we hear from God is when we take time away and retreat from life. To be sure, retreating for a time can be very valuable; but at least in this circumstance, God is encouraging the people to get moving. Moses is about to raise his staff and the waters are about to part.

You might think, "How easy to get moving when the water parts right before you." You're right: in this story, when God parted the waters, the decision to "go forward" was probably pretty obvious. But sometimes God gives us the first set of instructions and expects us to act on those without seeing a "parting of the waters." We see this in the story of Abraham when he sets off on his journey to a land that had not yet been identified. But he had his marching orders and he got a move on.

Hearing God's voice isn't a guaranteed thing. But today, if you would hear His voice, then you have a chance to trust in the Lord's leadership and respond in faith. You have a chance to see the salvation of the Lord, which He will accomplish for you today. And the Lord will fight for you while you "keep silent."

For that particular group long ago, those who were broken down along the shore of the Red Sea, God showed up, with crowbar in hand, and connected His tow truck to their story—and in so many words, told Pharaoh, "This isn't the way it's supposed to be." The Red Sea parted and the people passed through to safety. It was another chance for the students to get to know their teacher.

Was that it? Were those the only events where the people got to see God's work? No, there was more to come. Let's not let this well-known story, the parting of the Red Sea, overshadow the following, less-familiar parts of the narrative. For the students, the class orientation is over and the first of three tests is on its way. Let's follow them on their journey into the wilderness.

The First Test: Marah

As they continue on, the people pass through the waters of the Red Sea and travel three days' journey into the wilderness of Shur. This is where the students receive their first test, at a place called Marah (Exodus 15:22–27). The waters there are bitter; the name Marah means "bitter."[82] The name is a kind of warning sign that says, "Don't drink the water!"

When the people find out they can't drink the waters, they begin grumbling and complaining once again to Moses (Exodus 15:24). They don't cry out to the Lord at all—but Moses does on their behalf:

Then he cried out to the LORD, and the LORD showed him a tree; and he threw it into the waters, and the waters became sweet. (Exodus 15:25)

This tree, when it was applied to the waters, turned the waters of death into the waters of life. It was on the third day in the wilderness that a tree from the Lord brought their salvation.[83]

There He made for them a statute and regulation, and there He tested them. (Exodus 15:25b)

There it is, the first of the three tests. On their trip out of slavery, there was a lack of water and God tested the people by bringing them into a situation that they couldn't solve on their own. God wanted to see their response. That was the test. How did the students respond? They grumbled and complained. They failed the test. Yet God was still faithful.

Does God do this today? Does He allow situations in our life to occur that we can't solve on our own? Does He sometimes even lead us into these situations because they are our path out of Egypt? Yes, He does. He wants to see how we will respond. He's giving us a chance to develop faith in *His* plan instead of trying to create our own. We might not always think we deserve our situations or agree with God's response. That's OK. Remember, we are used to living outside the garden, and the way God does things might seem foreign at times. But He's the one who knows how things work best. He's the one that created the order and the function of the cosmos.[84]

Listen to God's faithful answer in this particular situation:

And He said, "If you will give earnest heed to the voice of the LORD your God, and do what is right in His sight, and give ear to His commandments, and keep all His statutes, I will put none of the diseases on you which I have put on the Egyptians; for I, the LORD, am your healer." (Exodus 15:26)

What does the beginning of this statement sound like? It sounds like we are back in Psalm 95:7: "Today if you would hear His voice . . ." It's the same prescription, but here it's stated this way: "If you will give earnest heed to the voice of the LORD your God . . ."

When you're given instruction from God and you've clearly heard His voice, if you follow His commands, this is what leads you into a deeper relationship of faith and toward your place of rest. If you don't . . . the biblical narrative suggests your heart will be hardened.

The Second Test: The Wilderness of Sin

The next story in the narrative takes place in the wilderness of Sin[85] (Exodus 16:1–21). Again, God has led the Israelites into a seemingly impossible situation. They didn't have enough food and the whole congregation grumbled and complained that Moses had brought them into the wilderness to die from hunger (Exodus 16:2). What was God's response?

> Then the LORD said to Moses, "Behold, I will rain bread from heaven for you; and the people shall go out and gather a day's portion every day, that I may test them, whether or not they will walk in My instruction." (Exodus 16:4)

There it is—the second test!

He provides both bread and quail for the people (Exodus 16:12) and gives them specific instructions regarding how much and when to collect the food He is providing (Exodus 16:16, 19). Some students passed the test, and some didn't.

Interestingly, these are the initial instructions for the observance of a seventh-day sabbath (Exodus 16:22–36). We mentioned back in chapter 2 that these instructions were given before the people received the Ten Commandments and the law at Mt. Sinai.

Let's remind ourselves again what the seventh-day sabbath is. It's a reminder of the restful rule experienced in the garden of Eden. That was when humanity first heard the voice of God, followed His instructions, and lived with Him at rest. Here, when the Lord tests the people a second time, He inserts instructions to remember the type of rest experienced in

Eden. God's telling them that the world of slavery they knew is not the way it is supposed to be. The teacher has something better to offer.

The Final Exam: Meribah and Massah

Then we arrive at the final exam: the events at Meribah and Massah (Exodus 17:1–7). Remember, this is the place that's codependently linked with Psalm 95 and Hebrews 3–4. It's *this* story that both of those scriptures use to make their point.

> Then all the congregation of the sons of Israel journeyed by stages from the wilderness of Sin, according to the command of the LORD, and camped at Rephidim, and there was no water for the people to drink. (Exodus 17:1)

God leads the people to a place where there was no water. Doesn't this test seem like one the teacher has given before? Yes, it does, and this time they have a chance to learn from the previous test and do better. They have a chance to trust God's plan and wait for His provision. But how did the people respond?

> Therefore, the people quarreled with Moses and said, "Give us water that we may drink." And Moses said to them, "Why do you quarrel with me? Why do you *test the* LORD?" (Exodus 17:2, emphasis mine)

And there it is, the final exam! But this time it's the *people* who tested *the Lord.* The students give the teacher an exam! The tables have turned. The proctor has flipped. And it's this response that kept the people from experiencing their rest, the Promised Land.[86]

> Then the LORD said to Moses, "Pass before the people and take with you some of the elders of Israel; and take in your hand your staff with which you struck the Nile, and go. Behold, I will stand

before you there on the rock at Horeb; and you shall strike the rock, and water will come out of it, that the people may drink." And Moses did so in the sight of the elders of Israel. (Exodus 17:5–6)

The people chose to grumble and complain, and it led to the hardening of their hearts. But did you notice that, despite their response, God was still faithful and provided exactly what they needed?

So what's significant about this event? Why is this event highlighted in both Psalm 95 and Hebrews 3–4? God had been gracious and faithful and gave the people a chance to learn from the previous tests and respond differently. But they didn't. Instead of choosing a faithful response of trusting God's plan and timing, they questioned Him the same way they had before and that's what flipped the tables. They developed a habit of questioning God and failed the final exam. That's why, this time, the students tested the teacher. That's Meribah and Massah, and it's this choice that prevented them from entering God's rest.

Today if you would hear His voice,

Do not harden your hearts,

As at Meribah, as in the day of Massah in the wilderness,

When your fathers tested Me,

They tried Me, though they had seen My work. (Psalm 95:7b–9)

Meribah—Forty Years Later

There is another Bible story that tells of water coming from a rock (Numbers 20:2–13). The name of that place is also called Meribah (but not Massah). While this may sound very similar,[87] it's an entirely different episode than the story in Exodus 17. It's in a different location and takes place nearly forty years later, but the similarity in name is a clue that the two events are codependently linked.

The first Meribah and Massah story (Exodus 17:1–7) involved the generation of people who came out of slavery in Egypt. This second Meribah involves their kids—the ones who watched their parents make poor decisions nearly every day. Those kids have now grown up and become the new wilderness generation, and they are just months away from following Joshua into the Promised Land.

What's the situation in Numbers 20? To cut to the chase, there was a lack of water. For Moses, who had seen God be faithful in this way at the beginning of their journey, and survived the last forty years in a desert without becoming dehydrated, this situation was a great opportunity to once again trust God's plan. But in this story, unbelief got the best of him.

> There was no water for the congregation, and they assembled themselves against Moses and Aaron. The people thus contended with Moses and spoke, saying, "If only we had perished when our brothers perished before the Lord! Why then have you brought the Lord's assembly into this wilderness, for us and our beasts to die here?" (Numbers 20:2–4)

Did you hear that? Grumble, grumble. Complain, complain. These kids are just like their parents!

God then tells Moses to assemble the congregation and take the rod (the same one used in the Exodus 17 story) with him. But instead of hitting the rock, Moses is supposed to only talk to the rock before the people (Numbers 20:8).

> So, Moses took the rod from before the Lord, just as He had commanded him; and Moses and Aaron gathered the assembly before the rock. And he said to them, "Listen now you rebels; shall we bring forth water for you out of this rock?" Then Moses lifted up his hand and struck the rock twice with his rod and water came forth abundantly, and the congregation and their beasts drank. (Numbers 20:9–11)

I think it's safe to say that Moses was a little hot, and in a fit of anger he disregarded God's instructions. Moses hits the rock not just once—he wanted to make sure everyone saw, so he hit it again!

And water poured forth from the rock.

But the LORD said to Moses and Aaron, "Because you have not believed Me, to treat Me as holy in the sight of the sons of Israel, therefore you shall not bring this assembly into the land which I have given them." (Numbers 20:12)

This is the episode that keeps Moses from entering God's rest, the Promised Land. It's because of his unbelief—his lack of faith. Sometimes my unbelief shows up in fits of anger too. Is that the case for you?

What about the generation of grown-up children? God gave them a test: no water to drink. That's an easy test to give when you live in a desert! Those kids grumbled and complained, and yet God was still faithful. It was a good chance for this new class of students to learn about the faithfulness of their teacher. That's how God works. Everyone must take their own set of tests, and God proves Himself faithful to every new generation. Every new class gets to see God work, learn who He is, and then decide for themselves how they will respond to His tests.

And the good news is: everyone can pass His class!

Let's Summarize

What are we supposed to learn from all these stories in Genesis, Exodus, and Numbers? Let's summarize the situation like this: Sin causes the world to live in a state of unrest. Humanity often doesn't listen to God's voice, and we try to solve the world's problems on our own.

But God has a plan. He has a way this thing is supposed to all work out. All He wants is for humanity to listen, hear His instruction, and get a move on. That's what rest is. It's not just believing, or listening, but *doing* what God says to do. That's part of the rest. That's living at rest with God, the true sabbath. It's having a place to be and a thing to do.

We should also expect God to test us on our path out of slavery—not just in one area of life, but in multiple areas. He might test you with food or water. If not those, it will be something else that's become important to you.

He might test you with finances. Does that ever happen? You might be tested in your relationships. Let me suggest a few. How about your relationship with your parents? Do you ever struggle with your parents? What about your children (those of you that have them)? What about the relationship with your siblings? Those are never a problem, are they? Neighbors? Coworkers? People on social media? That guy next to you at the stop light?

It's not only relationships. What about your plans for the future? Is God going to test you to respond in faith regarding your future? How about your physical health? If you haven't experienced that yet . . . just wait, you will. What about your employment? Are you going to trust God with His plans for your job? Do you think He will test you in that area?

I'm not sure how *you've* been tested. I only know the tests I've taken. That's the list I just shared with you. Those are the specific ways God has challenged me in my life. But I suspect you connected with parts of that list as well.

In the next chapter, I'll share an extended story of two of my tests. The first test came in my early twenties, and I failed it miserably! Then God tested me again, in a similar way, just before I turned forty. I'm happy to say I did much better the second time around. But again, more on those stories later.

Can we learn from God when he proves himself faithful? He will be faithful; it's His character. The next time a challenge pops up in a similar area of our life, how will we respond? That's the question. That's the warning. That's the test to see if we are able to remain restful, or if our hearts become more hardened in the process.

When we willingly fall under God's authority and trust Him with the circumstances of our lives, something interesting will begin to happen. He will have us apply a faithful response to areas in which He's never tested us before. A mature act of faith is learning to respond well in a new area of life. For instance, suppose God proved himself faithful early in your marriage in some unique way. You've learned to trust Him there, but then you have your first child. This is brand new for you. You've never been parents before. If you can take the faith lesson learned earlier in your marriage and immediately apply it to the first test you have regarding your children, you have the opportunity to remain in rest. God is inviting us to learn how to respond in faith to any new test that life may bring our way.

> So there remains a Sabbath rest for the people of God. For the one who has entered His rest has himself also rested from his works, as God did from His. Therefore, let us be diligent to enter that rest so that no one will fall, through following the same example of disobedience. (Hebrews 4:9–11)

Jesus Didn't Grumble

What does it look like to live *fully* at rest with God? In Exodus 14–17, we are given examples of how grumbling and complaining can keep us from experiencing God's rest. But as we discovered in chapter 4, humanity can look to Jesus and His ministry as a study guide for how to pass life's tests. Maybe the best example of this is the story of Jesus's temptation (testing) in the wilderness.[88]

The Gospel authors thematically link Jesus's baptism and testing in the wilderness (Matthew 3:13–4:11; Mark 1:9–13; Luke 3:21–4:13) to the events we've just studied in Exodus 14–17. In those Old Testament stories, we see Moses lead the people through the waters of the Red Sea, then into the wilderness where they are tested three times. These failed tests lead to forty years of wandering. Eventually, Joshua leads the second generation through the flood waters of the Jordan and into the Promised Land (Joshua 3:6–17).

In a similar progression of events, we see Jesus, one like Moses[89] and Joshua, also pass through the chaos waters of death. After Jesus's baptism in the Jordan, He immediately proceeds to the wilderness for a "period of forty." It's forty days, not years, but that doesn't matter; it's all a hyperlink back to the Old Testament stories. Then Jesus receives a trifecta of tests. Can you see that Jesus is thematically taking the tests that Israel failed? Let's take a closer look at these Old Testament parallels from Jesus's time in the wilderness, from Luke's account.

> Jesus, full of the Holy Spirit, returned from the Jordan and was led around by the Spirit in the wilderness for forty days. (Luke 4:1–2a)

Jesus is in the wilderness being led around by the Spirit. What does that sound like? It sounds an awful lot like a description of that first generation in Exodus. They too were led around in the wilderness by the Spirit of God. When you see something like that in the text—something with an obvious connection to an Old Testament story—you're not supposed to just skip over it. You're being invited to recognize the codependency. So just use your pencil and connect those dots.

> And He ate nothing during those days, and when they had ended, He became hungry. (Luke 4:2)

Do we know any stories from the Old Testament where people were wandering around in the wilderness, and then became hungry? Yup—it's taking us back to the grumblers and complainers who were hungry in Exodus 16.[90] Then, just like the hungry Hebrews, Jesus is given a test concerning food:

> And the devil[91] said to Him, "If You are the Son of God, tell this stone to become bread." And Jesus answered him, "It is written, 'Man shall not live on bread alone.'" (Luke 4:3–4)

How does Jesus pass the first test? He trusts the plan and reminds the devil of God's instructions in Scripture. But we need to see His response in its original context to fully understand what Jesus is saying. Who in the Old Testament said, "Man does not live on bread alone?" You might have already guessed: it was Moses. In fact, look at the larger context of that verse:

All the commandments that I am commanding you today you shall be careful to do, that you may live and multiply [something to do], and go in and possess the land [a place to be] which the LORD swore to give to your forefathers. You shall remember all the way in which the LORD your God has led you in the wilderness these forty years, that He might humble you, testing you, to know what was in your heart, whether you would keep His commandments or not. He humbled you and let you be hungry, and fed you with manna which you did not know, nor did your fathers know, that He might make you understand that man does not live by bread alone, but lives by everything that proceeds out of the mouth of the LORD. (Deuteronomy 8:1–3)

You may have noticed I added the "something to do" and "a place to be" notes into that verse. Did you notice anything else—the testing, the hunger, and the manna? When tested with hunger in the wilderness, Jesus doesn't grumble or complain. Rather, He quotes a passage that reminds everyone of God's faithful provision in Exodus 16. It's an example of learning from past faithfulness, and expecting the same faithfulness in the present. It's Jesus's way of saying, "God's plan is the best plan." It's a restful response.

Then the devil tests Jesus a second time.

And the devil said to Him, "I will give You all this domain and its glory; for it has been handed over to me, and I give it to whomever I wish. Therefore, if You worship before me, it shall all be Yours." Jesus answered him, "It is written, 'You shall worship the Lord your God and serve Him only.'" (Luke 4:6–9)

How does Jesus pass the second test? He reminds the devil of God's instructions given in Scripture. This time Jesus paraphrases from an earlier passage in Deuteronomy:

You shall fear only the LORD your God; and you shall worship Him and swear by His name. You shall not follow other gods, any of the gods of the peoples who surround you, for the LORD your God in the midst of you is a jealous God. (Deuteronomy 6:13–15)

Again, Jesus gives a faithful response. He does not grumble or complain. He reminds everyone of the instructions that had already been given. They are the instructions that describe how to remain at rest with God: worship Him only!

Then the devil tested Him a third time. And it's Jesus's final exam.

And he led Him to Jerusalem and had Him stand on the pinnacle of the temple, and said to Him, "If You are the Son of God, throw Yourself down from here; for it is written, 'He will command His angels concerning You to guard You,' and, 'On their hands they will bear you up, so that you will not strike Your foot against a stone.'" And Jesus answered and said to him, "It is said, 'You shall not put the Lord your God to the test.'" (Luke 4:9–12)

Did you notice, in this third test, that the devil started quoting Scripture—albeit out of context? This doesn't faze Jesus at all. How does He pass the final exam? He reminds Satan—and all of us—that we are not to test God. But there's also something Jesus *doesn't* say that is instrumental to His statement. Jesus doesn't quote the whole verse; He only says the first half of the sentence. And those familiar with this passage from Deuteronomy would have recognized the omission right away. So what is it that Jesus refers to, by not mentioning it?

You shall not put the Lord your God to the test, as you tested Him at Massah. (Deuteronomy 6:16)

Did you see that? By choosing this verse out of Deuteronomy, Jesus is intentionally hyperlinking back to the events of Exodus 17, at Meribah and Massah. You might have noticed that the name "Meribah" wasn't included above. Remember, there were two separate stories at places called Meribah (Exodus 17; Numbers 20), but only one of those can be described as where the people put the Lord to the test at Massah (Exodus 17).[92]

I find it interesting how often the story of Meribah and Massah is mentioned in the Old Testament (Deuteronomy 6:16; 9:22; 33:8; Psalm 81:7; 95:8). If we add in the times it also gets an indirect nod in the New Testament (Luke 4:12; Hebrews 3:15; 4:3, 5, 7), it becomes clear that there's an important lesson to be learned from the events at Meribah and Massah.

To pass *His* final exam in the wilderness, Jesus says, don't respond the way the wilderness generation did at Massah—when they failed *their* final exam. This masterful response concluded Jesus's trifecta of tests. Did you notice that He didn't grumble and complain during any of them? He responded in faith, fully convinced of the Father's character, trustworthiness, and ability to bring order and function to disorderly circumstances.

The Hebrews 3–4 passage spends a lot of time saying, "Don't do what they did. Don't respond the way they did at that place." In contrast, Jesus's temptation in the wilderness is a great example of exactly how we *should* respond. It's as if the teacher is saying, "OK students, follow me in my response to the tests that life brings. You have a faithful God who is worthy of your trust . . . here's how to pass the tests."

ADDITIONAL REST RESOURCES

CHAPTER 7

TESTING THE WATERS OF REST

All who have once or twice experienced the power of God, and distrust it for the future, are convicted of unbelief.

—John Calvin[93]

Here we are, at the final chapter. And just as God rested on the *seventh* day of creation, I feel it's appropriate for a book about biblical rest to conclude with a *seventh* chapter.

What have we accomplished so far? Well, in six chapters we gave order and function to the topic of rest. We took the chaos that exists around the idea of sabbath, and gave everything a place to be and something to do.

First, we put the seventh-day rest God experienced in Genesis in its rightful, and defining, place at the beginning. Then we allowed that restful "never-ending-functional rule" to give structure and meaning to all the other conversations we've had about rest.

We then put the reminders of rest in their proper place: in the domain of the biblical shadows. We now know that's where they belong, and we've correctly identified their thing to do: they remind us of the restful rule of Eden, and point forward to the ministry of the "new Joshua."

Following that, we looked at the New Testament's presentation of Jesus. This allowed us to position His ministry of rest appropriately at the top of the list. He's not only the human yoked alongside us showing us our restful work, but also the very God who originally defined rest, created it, and guarantees its survival. It took six chapters to get our understanding of rest properly placed and functioning.

Thus, there was evening, and there was morning for six chapters. In this way the concepts surrounding rest were completed, in all their hosts. By the seventh chapter, we completed the work on rest that we had done, and now we rest, in this seventh chapter, from all the work we have done. Now God will bless this seventh chapter, and sanctify it, because in it we will find rest from all the work we have done.

OK . . . I hope you recognized that last bit as a corny adaptation of the seventh day of creation. Forgive me for taking that much license, but I wanted to make it clear that this chapter is all about entering into rest. It's a different type of rest. And let's hope it is, because all our previous efforts have left us wanting, wandering, and wondering where we went wrong.

Back in the Neighborhood

In the opening chapter, I suggested that biblical rest is a neighborhood of highly interconnected streets. When we are able to back away from our current cul-de-sac conversations and see the whole neighborhood of rest, that's when we begin to understand what God means when He offers "rest."

I'm guessing this neighborhood is bigger than you originally expected it to be. Rest is woven into the biblical story from beginning to end. It's a very large network of concepts, ideas, and themes. You might be excited to share what you've learned, and yet intimidated about walking someone else down these streets. How might we introduce such a large labyrinth to those who are stuck in the cul-de-sac of the seventh day? Just start at the beginning, and walk them down one street at a time. That's what we've done *here*, and you can do the same *out there*.

But there's a part of this neighborhood we haven't visited. It's where you live. It's your own personal residence, the story of how God has shown Himself faithful in your life. When we articulate our personal stories, that's when the road map to sabbath rest begins to really make sense. So that's what I'll do in the pages that remain. I'll share pieces of my story, invite you to consider your own, and share how these concepts could completely change the way we think and live.

Sweet Spots

In chapter 4, we discovered that Jesus's "yoke of rest" is not an invitation to idleness. It's really a call to action, utilizing a brand-new guidance system. When we attach ourselves to Jesus, and His yoke, He leads us to places we're supposed to be. And when we get there, its Jesus's yoke that suggests to us the activities we are supposed to be doing. But what does it practically look like when someone is yoked to Jesus? Let's explore this in a little more detail.

Most who will read this book are very talented people. As members of humanity, each of us have been given abilities we enjoy and in which we excel. Our talents can be displayed in many different forms. Someone can be talented athletically, musically, artistically, or organizationally, just to name a few. Talent can spring forth in many ways. But no matter who we are, each of us has areas in our lives to which we are naturally drawn. Because we are members of humanity, and creatures created in the image of God, all of us have these "sweet spots."

Sweet spots are those things we do, that when we do them it's like, "Oh yeah! That's what I was made to do!" I don't know what that thing is for you. I know what it is for me. I experience that feeling when I teach. When I finish presenting something, I'm usually exhausted because I've been working hard. But because I've been where I'm supposed to be and I've been doing what I'm supposed to be doing, when I finish I get totally amped up but I'm also exhausted. That's a great feeling! It's one of the best experiences in life. That's me when I'm at rest.

Have you experienced something like that in your own life? Maybe that happens when you're creating a song, maybe it hits you after finishing a piece of artwork, or maybe you planned a large event and when it was finished you felt the full satisfaction of a job well done. I don't know what it is for you, but I know there is something that you were made to do, and when you're done doing it you just know, "That's my sweet spot."

The problem is that many of us get caught working in the curse-a-day world, outside the garden, and far away from any sweet spot we may have.

There is nothing worse than being unfulfilled in the work that we do, but that's just the unfortunate reality for so many. When we find ourselves there, the real question is, how do we get back under the rule and authority of God? How do we find rest in a restless world of chaos and hurt? How do we find our sweet spot within God's restful rule, and function the way we're supposed to?

The offer of sabbath rest that Jesus gives is an offer to be in a continual search for that place. And since it's a search within our sweet spots, it's not a worry-driven "have to" obligation. Rather, the search can become an exciting "get to" opportunity. There is nothing more freeing than God saying, "I created you for good works and I've given you a very particular set of skills.[94] Now, let's go see where and how you might be able to use your talents."

Remember the imperative from Hebrews, "He again fixes a certain day, 'Today,' saying . . . 'Today if you hear His voice . . .'" (Hebrews 4:7). What day is the sabbath? Hebrews 4 says, "It's today!" And the good news is: it's always "today"!

Jesus's offer of sabbath rest is not a one-day-a-week ceasing of activity. He offers the sabbath as a daily opportunity to hear the voice of God and respond in faith. If you listen for it, you'll hear Him invite you to places you've never been, and to consider doing things you've never done. He will offer unexpected situations that give the opportunity to use the talents He's already supplied. If you do hear His voice, the only question left is, "How will you respond?" Will you trust Him to lead you to a new place, or will you offer your version of "Grumble, grumble, complain, complain"?

Moving Targets

Another favorite movie of mine is *Napoleon Dynamite*. It's a great show full of enough one-liners to repeat one a day for a whole year. I also like it because the movie's talented lead actor, Jon Heder, attended a high school in my hometown! But it's a different character from the story with whom I most easily identify. In the movie, Uncle Rico is a rather awkward middle-aged man who is consumed by a desire to go back in time. No, this is not a science fiction movie—Uncle Rico just can't get past the fact that his high school football team lost the state championship game his senior year. Evidently, he was the team's backup quarterback and he thinks he would have played well if he had only been given the chance. He wholeheartedly believes that if his coach would have played him in the fourth quarter of that game, they would have won state. In his own words, "We would've been state champions. No doubt. No doubt in my mind."

Uncle Rico spends the better part of the movie practicing his football skills and talking about "winning state." Sadly, that part of his life is in the rear-view mirror, and there isn't any turning around. For Uncle Rico, high school football was a sweet spot. When he was the backup quarterback, he was in his place and doing his thing. When that was over, he just had a hard time pivoting to find a new sweet spot. He didn't realize that, just like the second-string receivers he threw passes to in practice, sweet spots are moving targets.

Our "sweet spots" can change as time goes by. If I was able to take you back in time, we would see that in high school and college, I spent a lot of time in athletic endeavors. I trained for hours upon hours by throwing, catching, and bouncing spheres covered in cowhide. That was a big part of my life for many years—and just like Uncle Rico, I too never won a state title! Eventually the time came when my athletic opportunities came to an end; the ACL (anterior cruciate ligament) in my right knee snapped, and the competitive athletic part of my life was largely over.

This is about the same time I pivoted into teaching. When I got that first job teaching junior high and coaching, I knew it was exactly where

I was supposed to be. I just knew it. It was a new sweet spot for me. But then, after three short years, my circumstances changed again with a job offer back in my hometown. That's when I started selling real estate, and it was a very strange transition for me. I originally had no idea I would end up in that profession. I'll share the story of this transition later in more detail. It was a restless part of my search for rest. But eventually, I found out that selling real estate back in my hometown was exactly where I was supposed to be. And then for a long time, fifteen years, that was a sweet spot.

But then 2008 happened. Do you remember back when the whole US economy just shut down for a few years? I didn't realize it at first, but God was beginning to say, "Real estate was your place to be . . . but now I've got somewhere else for you." Through life's circumstances, He was communicating that it was time to start looking for a new place to be. At that time in my life, I remember thinking, "What else is there that I could do?" I just couldn't see my next pivot.

Those circumstances began the unlikely transition to being a full-time pastor. And, I've got to be honest, those first few years of being a pastor were terribly awkward. It wasn't due to how I was treated at the church; the people there were wonderful to me. I just didn't feel like I was a pastor. It didn't feel like who I was. I had been an athlete, and a teacher, and a real estate agent, but I'd never been a pastor before. Yet even in *that* role, I eventually found my footing, and God confirmed that's where I was supposed to be.

Several years after I became a pastor, God called me out of that position and again put me on a new search. That's where I find myself today. I'm once again looking for the place that God desires me to be. I'm searching for the thing He would have me doing at this time in my life. I'm pivoting.

In his book *The Second Mountain*, David Brooks describes what he believes to be the difference between a *career* and a *vocation*. He suggests careers are often chosen based on the highest return on one's investment of time and effort, and potential for upward mobility. But a vocation is a different type of calling. Vocations are often sparked by an annunciation moment, where something delights you and you become entranced by that thing. He describes it this way:

> In the vocation mentality, you're not living on the ego level of your consciousness—working because the job pays well or makes life convenient. You're down in the substrate. Some activity or some injustice has called to the deepest level of your nature and demanded an active response.... Often people feel a call but don't really understand it. The summons to vocation is a very holy thing. It feels mystical, like a call from deep to deep. But then the messy way it happens in actual lives doesn't feel holy at all; just confusing and screwed up.[95]

God often leads us into situations that reveal our sweet spots. This can be one way He calls us to a vocation. As I look back on all the transitions I just described, most of the time I had no idea what I was doing. I often felt like a round peg trying to fit into a square hole. But each time, I felt like I was answering a call of some sort or another. Most of the transitions I've made throughout my life have had a little of that awkward stage. I think that's normal.

Sometimes a vocation can blossom into a personal ministry. We've all heard of someone who volunteers at, or maybe even creates, a nonprofit organization based on a vocational calling. It's also true that a person's vocation can even develop into a career. While a vocational career might seem like an ideal situation, it can also be a complicated marriage. When I became a pastor, at one level it was a vocational calling. But when I decided to also make it my career, I created a Venn-diagram-type situation where the two intersected. While my vocation and career often overlapped, sometimes my career obligated me to responsibilities that weren't a part of my vocational call. To the extent one can successfully negotiate these differences, a vocational career can be a very rewarding situation.

Testing the Waters of Rest

After several knee surgeries in my twenties, I began competing in "sprint triathlons." These are races where the entrants swim a short distance, ride a bike as fast as they can for a few miles, and then run like the wind to the finish line. These exercises were good rehab for my previously injured appendages. But a cursory review of my finishing times in these "sprint triathlons" might suggest I never actually "sprinted" at all. In my first race, I rode a mountain bike with big knobby tires. The bike also had a full set of fenders that acted like spinnakers as I rode. I rode so slowly that I recall three small children laughing at me as they rolled past on their Big Wheels!

My decision to become a triathlete caused me to spend many hours in the local swimming pool. I had taken summer swimming lessons in my youth, but had never learned the art of breathing between strokes without swallowing lots of air. It took me about six weeks to master that process. Once I figured that out, I grew to love all my time training in the water. Well, I enjoyed everything except one thing. It's one aspect of swimming I still don't enjoy to this day.

I hate getting into cold water!

I've never really gotten used to the initial shock of the water quickly changing my body's temperature. My disdain for this has caused me to develop a slow and calculated routine for entering these frigid ponds. I begin by putting only one foot in the water as I sit on the side of the pool. Then I slowly slide my second foot in alongside the first. After several moments (which I spend pretending I'm stretching), I'll splash some water on the rest of my legs, and then a little on my upper body. Eventually I put my swimming cap and goggles in place, notify my watch that a workout is about to begin, and launch into the water.

That's my routine. That's how I test the waters of the pool, en route to fully committing the entirety of my epidermis. It's just one foot at a time.

This is similar to the routine we might have when testing the waters of rest. God will bring new opportunities into our lives and say, "Trust me." But unfamiliar waters are often too risky to fully commit to in one jump. These are chances to dip our foot into situations we wouldn't normally choose on our own.

God does this for each of us. He's given each of us talents and abilities, and He brings people across our path who offer the chance to further explore our gifts. They often present themselves as "unexpected encounters" that leave us asking, "Why did I just have *that* conversation, with *that* person?" It's what God does for us. He leads us to unexpected encounters to get us thinking outside our little boxes. This is one of the ways He leads people back to their place of rest.

This process of following God into rest might seem like it should be more natural and comfortable. But these places are often awkward. Rest under God's rule and authority doesn't always take us to the places we would naturally choose. We are used to working, and making decisions, outside the rule of the garden. So when God invites you back into His space, don't be surprised when it awkwardly leads to unexpected places.

How do we find opportunities to test those waters? We listen for God's voice and step out in faith when He brings something across our doorstep. All we need to say is, "I'm willing to test these waters. I'm willing to sit down and dip one of my feet in that situation."

Sometimes the things we try are a perfect fit and we can just jump in and start swimming laps. But sometimes the things we try don't work out. I've tested so many situations where I got one or two feet into the water and it turned out to be all wrong. That's totally OK. In fact, I'm convinced sometimes that's exactly what God wants. He wants us to dip our foot into those waters, and then right back out again. It's often the lessons we learn in these testing situations that teach us new things about ourselves. They sometimes reveal skills that were previously unknown. They get us out of our comfort zone and trusting God.

You're about to finish this book. Soon you'll put it down and be faced with the reality of the world in which you live. What is God's offer of rest for you? It doesn't even need to be your full-time anything. It could be something you do once a week, once a month, or even one time a year. Let's also be willing to move our thinking outside the four walls of our church buildings. God's doing a lot of good work within the walls we've constructed, but I'm convinced He's doing the majority of His work outside of those boxes. There are lots of places to be and things to do in God's great big world.

The author Bob Goff summarizes our opportunity this way: "Every day, God invites us on an adventure. It's not a trip where He sends us a rigid itinerary, He simply invites us. God asks what it is He's made us to love, what it is that captures our attention, what feeds that deep indescribable need of our souls to experience the richness of the world He made. And then, leaning over us, He whispers, 'Let's go do that together.'"[96]

What kind of waters has God brought you to lately? I invite you to test the waters of rest. For some of you, just as you've been reading this section you're already thinking about something you thought you might try. You've already been reminded of a conversation you had last week, something God has put on your heart, or an opportunity you know is in your sweet spot but maybe a little outside your comfort zone. Maybe it hasn't even been a sweet spot for you in the past, but maybe it could be.

Thank God He calls us outside our comfort zones. That's how we grow.

I encourage you to share this journey with those you trust. Get support from people who know you well. Seek out others who encourage you to explore your place to be. Find folks who are searching for their thing to do. Much of rest is the search to find and the opportunity to display God's rule in a world that so desperately needs to see it in action.

So, today if you hear His voice . . . be willing to test the waters of rest.

Warning Passages

The book of Hebrews is famous for its warning passages. Let's look at one warning in Hebrews 3 regarding rest, and notice the sense of urgency it describes:

> Take care, brethren, that there not be in any one of you an evil, unbelieving heart that falls away from the living God. (Hebrews 3:12)

And just a few verses later, "So we see that they were not able to enter because of unbelief. Therefore, let us fear if, while a promise remains of entering His rest, any one of you may seem to have come short of it" (Hebrews 3:19–4:1).

Is it possible for a *believer* in Christ to be denied godly rest because of *unbelief*? On the surface, that question might seem like a contradiction. How can someone be a believer and also have unbelief? The author of Hebrews suggests this is more than a hypothetical situation—it's a real possibility.

> Therefore, let us be diligent to enter that rest, so that no one will fall, through following the same example of disobedience. (Hebrews 4:11)

Hebrews suggests that believers can come short of entering rest through some sort of disobedience. What type of disobedience? The kind of grumbling and complaining we saw at Meribah and Massah.

What does it mean for modern-day believers when they, for whatever reason, don't enter God's rest? Is Jesus's offer of rest an all-or-nothing situation, or is it something different? This is a big theological question[97] for sure. I don't plan on considering all the nuances here, but we must at least consider a few ideas.

First, to better understand the question, let's focus on the original wilderness generation and ask, "What did it mean for *those* people when they didn't enter into God's rest?" Remember the picture of entering into rest for this group was the offer of physically entering the Promised Land. To be sure, their lack of faith prevented them from entering God's rest, but did that end their relationship with God?

Some people might say yes. They read about some of God's responses and want to conclude that He wouldn't respond that way with people He loved. For example, God sent a plague on the people (Numbers 16:41–50), sent killer snakes into their camp (Numbers 21:6), and swallowed up whole families with "holy sinkholes" (Numbers 16:28–33). It might

seem from these examples that God wasn't interested in further develop-
ing His relationship with these people. But those examples alone don't
present the whole picture.

Let's remember that every day, for the entire forty years in the wilderness, God provided manna for the people to eat. Every week God built
in a relationship-building exercise: they collected a double portion on the
sixth day and didn't collect manna on the seventh. This is certainly a picture of an ongoing relationship.

We know that God was guiding them by the pillar of fire by night
and the cloud by day during their time in the desert (Exodus 13:21–22;
Psalm 78:14; 1 Corinthians 10:1–4). Also, throughout the entire forty
years He was guiding them, daily, from the middle of their camp (Numbers 2:1–2).

As we look at these examples, we realize that the people's inability
to have a faithful response didn't automatically end their relationship
with God. But we also know that their unfaithful responses significantly
changed the quality of their relationship.

When that generation failed to enter the Promised Land, they missed
out on a restful-relationship opportunity. I don't mean they missed out
on some "quality hammock time" in the land. Their unfaithful response
caused them to miss out on living in the land at peace with God. Instead
of that existence, their relationship with God took place in the wilderness. Just think about what a difference this represents. The Promised
Land is described as a place where there were already fully developed cit-
ies, homes supplied with everything they would need, plenty of water,
and vineyards that had already been planted (Deuteronomy 6:10–11).
Instead of that life, God faithfully provided for them in the barren waste-
land instead.

It's this example we must apply to our own lives. Jesus has in mind
a place for each of us. To be clear, this is not a promise to provide fancy
clothes, an expensive car, or a big house. Those things are not bad in and
of themselves, and it's fine if you experience some of them along your
path. But God's promises concern so much more than those temporary

indicators of worldly success. God is more concerned with the condition of your soul. We've all known people with enough money to buy anything they want but who are unable to purchase the rest that their soul desires.

If we hear Him and trust Him, we can follow Him into that place of rest and experience His provision for us. But if we don't hear, or don't trust, and in turn don't follow His direction, He won't abandon us. He will still be faithful, but it could be a significantly different experience for us than the one He had originally prepared.

How are you doing with these components of rest? Maybe you feel a previous life decision has landed you in a place you aren't supposed to be. You might be terribly weary from living where you are, but don't despair. You are not doomed to forty years of personal-wilderness wandering. Remember Jesus's offer:

Come to me, all you who are weary and heavy-laden, and I will give you rest. Take my yoke upon you and learn from Me, for I am gentle and humble in heart, and you will find rest for your souls. For My yoke is easy and My burden is light. (Matthew 11:28–30)

Today is the day, no matter where you currently find yourself, to find His yoke, attach yourself to it, and begin following his directions to rest.

Is Sabbath Street Straight?

What does it realistically look like to experience this type of rest? The Bible, as a whole, presents Moses as an example of both unbelief and great faith.

But the LORD said to Moses and Aaron, "Because you have not believed Me . . . therefore you shall not bring this assembly into the land which I have given them." (Numbers 20:12)

This passage highlights Moses's unbelief, but there are many other Scriptures that suggest that he was a man of great faith. In the New

Testament, Hebrews 11 is often referred to as the "faith chapter" because it gives several Old Testament examples of faithful people. In that chapter, Moses is given more space than any other character (Hebrews 11:23–29). The author of Hebrews spends considerable time recounting many of the faithful events of Moses's life, but there is something interesting at the end of these verses:

> By faith they passed through the Red Sea as though they were passing through dry land; and the Egyptians, when they attempted it, were drowned. (Hebrews 11:29)

Did you notice? That last verse lumps Moses in with the whole wilderness generation that came out of Egypt. They—everyone who passed through the Red Sea that day—are lifted up as examples of great faith. And yet the same author wrote about those same people in Hebrews 3–4, and there chose to highlight their unbelief.

Both Moses and those he led out of slavery are described as having great faith *and* extraordinary unbelief. They are examples of great faith . . . and at the same time they are examples of how not to respond.

Without meaning to be pretentious at all, this sounds a bit like me. In fact, it sounds a bit like everyone who has faith. A trip down Sabbath Street is not always as straight a path as we would like. We will have moments of great faith, where our decision to trust God allows us to exist in an unhindered relationship with Him. These are often followed by moments of varying levels of unbelief that pull us in and out of that garden relationship. Real life shows us that these two realities are often, and unfortunately, seamlessly stitched.

The Dimmer Switch of Faith

Some would like to define unbelief as a "lack of any faith," but I like to think about faith in terms of a dimmer switch. I'm talking about the switches that control light fixtures. There are many different styles, but they all have the same two basic functions. The ones we have at our house have a toggle switch at the bottom. What does that toggle switch do? It's a feature that turns the power on and off.

The other feature is the dimmer part of the switch. This is usually a knob that slides up and down. It allows the light fixture to display light at varying levels. It's this feature that you have to tell young children to keep their hands off, because it's really fun to play with. If you move the dimmer switch up, the light is bright. If you slide it down, you'll have a hard time finding your way through the room.

The important thing to remember is this: If the toggle switch is off, it doesn't matter what you do with the dimmer switch. But when the toggle switch is on, then the power is routed to the dimmer and the light can come through at many different levels.

I like to think of faith in this way. One aspect of faith is like the toggle switch; it's either on or off. You either have it or you don't.

But let's consider the story of Moses that we've been following in this study. He's a character who faithfully followed God for many years, yet in that one episode in Numbers 20 he's described as a man without faith. People tend to think of faith as an all-or-nothing commodity. Do you have faith? Yes . . . or no. In one sense, you can talk about faith in that "toggle-switch" type way, but I think faith is much more complicated than that.

Jesus talks about faith in terms not only of existence (yes or no), but of quantity and quality as well. There are times He refers to people of "little faith" (Matthew 6:30; 8:26; 14:31; 16:18; 17:20), and at other times he describes people of "great faith" (Matthew 8:10; 15:28). Those seem like dimmer-switch descriptions.

I like to think the Bible presents faith as more than just an on/off switch. When we hear the description of Moses as a man who acted in unbelief, we are probably misreading that if we think of him as a man who's completely void of faith. Rather, I think we're just reading a description of a moment in his life when the toggle switch is on, but the dimmer is way down to the bottom.

Are you a person with the toggle switch on . . . or off? If it's off, then stop playing with the dimmer switch! It won't do anything. For you, it's time to focus on the toggle switch and consider becoming a person of faith in Christ.

Once that toggle has been flipped, what can we expect through life? We should expect times of "great faith" where that dimmer switch is all the way up, the lights are bright, and we are seeing how God works in our life very clearly. Then, right around the corner from that experience, we might find ourselves with the dimmer switch down.

We need to know that just because there doesn't seem to be any juice coming through to the light, that doesn't mean the toggle switch is off. This is the picture of faith the Bible gives, and it's much more complicated than we sometimes make it out to be.

So what does it mean for someone to not enter into rest? For those in our Old Testament example it was a qualitatively different relationship with God, but because their toggle switch had been flipped, it was still a relationship. Instead of enjoying the land and the freedom that it offered, they were led around the wilderness. Instead of gathering every type of food the land would have provided, they got up every morning, collected manna, and drank water. They were on a bread-and-water diet. This is the qualitative difference between a restful relationship with God and one characterized by mistrust.[98]

So, if Moses is an example of sometimes displaying "great faith," but at other times "little faith," to whom can we turn to see a perfect example? Well, we already know the answer to that question, but let's allow the Bible to answer it one more time. The faith chapter, Hebrews 11, is immediately followed by this statement at the beginning of chapter 12:

> Therefore, since we have so great a cloud of witnesses surrounding us, let us also lay aside every encumbrance and the sin which so easily entangles us, and let us run with endurance the race that is set before us, fixing our eyes on Jesus, the author and perfecter of faith. (Hebrews 12:1–2a)

Once again, Jesus is the correct answer to the question! He is the One with no deficiencies. It's His example of mature faith that leads to a life fully at rest with God.

My Personal Story

I've chosen to close with a personal story that illustrates a portion of my journey into rest. I began teaching about biblical rest, in bits and pieces, in 2006. It's been a long journey of study for me, and an equally long path to effective application in my life. My wife and I have been challenged to insert what we've learned into practical situations life has presented over the years. While we've certainly not yet arrived at perfection, this study has greatly changed the way we look at opportunities for rest. It has also changed the way we've responded to some challenges life has thrown our way. Here's a defining example from our story.

Right out of college I taught junior high English for three years in Washington State. Then we moved back to Salem, Oregon, where I sold real estate for a while, and then I eventually became a pastor. It was the opportunity to work at my father-in-law's real estate firm, back in my hometown, that drew me out of that initial teaching job in Washington. So Lisa and I moved from Tacoma, Washington back to Salem, where we had both grown up.

This was such a major change in direction for me that we decided to officially just take a year's leave of absence from my school district job, just in case things didn't work out. We thought I might want to go back and continue teaching at my old job.

I don't know if you are aware of this, but while teachers don't get paid a lot, they do receive a steady paycheck with healthcare benefits. When we moved to Salem and I began selling real estate, it took me a few months to figure something out:

If you don't sell anything, the company doesn't pay you.

Let me just say that my first year did not go well. I didn't sell anything in the first nine months. My gracious father-in-law had extended a line of credit for us to use for living expenses until I got my career established. This seemed like a great idea when we didn't owe him any money . . . so we signed up. That first year, because I wasn't selling anything, we accumulated about $24,000 in debt on that credit line.

You need to understand that the year prior, as a teacher, I had made $21,900. So, in my mind, we were in debt by more than a full year's income. Even though we limited our expenditures to basic living and some business expenses, we were digging a hole pretty fast for our family.

I was doing everything I knew how to do. This was still in the early days of the internet, so I was forced to beat the bushes using some of the more traditional sales methods. I cold-called people on the phone, using a reverse directory. I walked neighborhoods and knocked on random doors, just hoping to find someone that was thinking about buying or selling a house. I was holding open houses almost every Saturday and Sunday.

It was awful.

It was bad mostly because nothing was working. It was the first time in my life where I honestly put my full effort into something and didn't get any favorable results. It was rather frustrating, to say the least. And for the first time in my life, I began to slip into a deep depression. I struggled to get out of bed—not just in the morning but all day. It got so I didn't want to face another day at work.

I began to wonder if I ever should have left my teaching job back in Tacoma. I asked myself questions like, "Did we move back to Salem a little too fast?" I said to Lisa, "Do you remember back in Tacoma when we had a steady paycheck . . . with healthcare included?"

I began to romanticize the place we had been. Does that sound familiar at all? The people that came out of Egypt had a similar response.[99]

About nine months into my new career, the time was approaching for me to give the school district an answer regarding my year's leave of absence. I had to let them know whether I was going to return to teaching. Lisa and I wondered whether or not we should try to stick it out in my new job in Salem.

We agreed we would pray about the situation. Those prayers sounded something like this: "God, I've tried everything I know to do to solve this situation we're in. Four weeks from now, unless you present something better, we think returning to Tacoma is our best option. If we do that, we will just have to slowly pay back our debt as best we can."

That's what we prayed. How depressing!

I'm not sure if you recognized it, because I hid it within the language of my prayer, but that was me grumbling and complaining. I may have dressed my language up in its Sunday best, but I was letting God know that He had made a mistake, and that I had a better plan. It was my bite of the forbidden fruit.

But about two weeks into our "month of prayer," the home builder for whom I had been conducting open houses unexpectedly expanded their business and bought building lots in a second subdivision. I inherited a few listings in the old subdivision because their agent moved to the new location.

It was during one of their open houses, in the third week, that I met a couple who was interested in building a house. I sat that couple down with the builder. They agreed on a price and I wrote up a sales agreement.

It was in the fourth week that I wrote two more offers.

We had given God a four-week time limit. During that span, I wrote enough business that, when it eventually closed, we were able to pay off our entire line of credit. And with some additional sales that followed, we were eventually able to deposit a large amount of savings in the bank.

At the end of these four weeks, Lisa and I looked at each other and said, "What . . . just . . . happened?" We had been looking at each other for the nine months just prior to that wondering what was happening. Then God, in a way we could not have imagined possible, miraculously proved himself faithful in the area of finances in our lives. I would have been happy with enough money to pay off only half the debt, but that's not how God answered.

Well, things went pretty well for the next twelve years. We had a great real estate market during that time, but then 2008 showed up.

That's the year several parts of the financial sector fell apart over a relatively short period of time. As a result, people couldn't get loans as easily as they had before. They couldn't get loans to buy houses. They couldn't get loans to build houses. This is not good news if you happen to be a real estate agent.

Within two or three months, everything in my line of work quickly ground to a halt.

Lisa and I had saved some money because we had lived on less than we made for several years. There were about six months where I tried everything I knew to do to create more business. But the market had changed so much that nothing was working.

Does this sound familiar at all? The circumstances were dramatically different than the first time, but it was eerily familiar for us. That's the way it is when God puts impossible situations in your life. The circumstances may be dramatically different, but parts of the test will seem very familiar.

Once again, having tried everything we knew to do, Lisa and I had a decision to make. We saw that our savings was running out. We were in another financial crisis that we weren't able to solve on our own.

So let me ask a question: Based on everything you've read in this book, what two options did we have in regard to our response to these new circumstances? We could have grumbled and complained—but this time, a new choice was available because of the way God had miraculously responded in faithfulness the first time. We could trust in God's faithfulness and wait for His plan and timing to be revealed. By this time in our lives, I had already discovered the lessons out of Hebrews 3–4, and I had been teaching them to others in many different settings. So that created a little more pressure.

Lisa and I sat down and we literally said, "OK, we have a choice. How are we going to respond?" And here is the prayer we came up with:

"God, we have no idea how you are going to solve this one, but we trust that you can. We will keep working, doing everything we know to do along the way, but we will have our eyes and ears open anticipating an unexpected solution. We will wait and trust for your timing."

That's as close as we could come to a "Jesus response" out of *His* temptation story. Let's wait for God and expect something miraculous to happen.

About three weeks after saying that prayer, I got a call from a pastor who I had helped purchase a house a few years before. We had developed a friendship. He had offered me a job at the church several times when the real estate market was doing better. My response had always half-jokingly been "Oh Pastor, you can't afford me."

This time I heard his voice on the other end of the line. He asked, like he always did, "When are you going to come work for me?" I actually said to him, "Pastor, I think you can afford me now!"

Over the next two months I accepted a full-time pastoral position at that church. During that time, I also began talking to agents in my real estate firm about possibly purchasing my company. That doesn't usually happen in a down real estate market, but that's exactly what happened.

About six months into my new job at the church, I finalized the sale of my real estate company to a group of those agents.

Just like the first time, God's solution was quite unexpected. I didn't ever envision myself ending up on a church staff. But our response this time led to a completely different experience for Lisa and me. This time we had a hopeful prayer, and we expected God to be faithful.

I can only describe it as restful.

We experience rest as we fall under the authority of the One who has more control than we do. And thank God that He does. How ironic is it that godly rest isn't about taking time off from work, but rather trusting God to lead us into the work He's created us to do?

What's the Question?

One question I've heard is "How has God shown Himself faithful in your life?" I've just shared one example from my story, but that's not the only time Lisa and I experienced God's faithfulness—not even close! I know if you're a person of faith, and have been walking with the Lord for any amount of time, you have your own stories of God's faithful work in your life.

What are the areas in which He's tested you? What was your response when He tested you? What could your response be in the future? Could it be different . . . better . . . more restful?

I briefly mentioned it earlier, but I think it's appropriate to repeat it again: "According to Hebrews 4:7, what day is sabbath rest available to the believer if they hear God's voice?"

The answer is "today," and it's always today.! No matter when you are reading this, it's the sabbath! So today, if you hear His voice, do not harden your heart. Rather, let your heart become softened by the faithfulness of God, and trust Him enough to fall under His functional rule.

ADDITIONAL
REST
RESOURCES

AFTERWORD

THE EIGHTH DAY

The bulk of this book has been dedicated to rethinking our understanding of biblical rest. We now understand that godly rest is not a lazy day in a hammock. It's really the ceasing of our own attempts to rule, and our active engagement in the world using the gifts and talents God has given us. When we rule, subdue, cultivate, and keep within God's plan, we can experience the rest that's available through Christ.

In chapter 1, I suggested that God's restful rule continued past the seventh day of creation on into the eighth day, the ninth, and so on. God's rest has never ended. And if, as the author of Hebrews suggests, a believer's rest is similar, it's important to explore some practical ways that we can stretch our rest as well to an eighth day, a ninth day, and beyond. So, before we close, let's extend the neighborhood metaphor a little and consider some simple practices that can help us safely avoid the common distractions, dead ends, and dangerous situations often found on the streets of sabbath.

Resetting toward Rest

Our new understanding of rest will require us to periodically reset toward rest. Why would we need to develop a routine of resetting our focus back to rest? It's because the curse-a-day world is continually trying to pull us off course. And one wrong turn can greatly affect our destination. What does a reset look like? Well, there's a lot of flexibility in how one might implement this concept, but at a minimum, it should be a regular examination of where you are, what you've been doing, what God's recently put on your plate, and careful consideration of your next steps in the process. Let's remind ourselves of some of the points we've covered.

In chapter 7, I suggested that each of us has sweet spots in our life: areas where God has gifted us. Within these spaces, we experience true joy. Part of a reset toward rest is the continual search for meaningful activity within these spots. It is recognizing they are mobile and changing, and thus will require our willingness to pivot, when necessary, to be able to utilize them. But remember, we are not on our own in this search. When we attach ourselves to Jesus's yoke, the Holy Spirit guides us along the way. All we need to do is pay attention and know what to look for.

The longer I live, the better I become at recognizing when God's communicating. He sometimes speaks through my study of Scripture. At other times He uses the people around me who I know and trust. But more and more, I'm finding He communicates to me through unexpected events. God often brings me into situations that at first seem to happen by chance, often through conversations with people I've never met. Someone will present a need, offer a service, introduce me to a new concept, or connect several ideas. I used to just chalk these situations up to coincidence, but now I sometimes recognize them as God's voice.

And I know I'm not alone. Every day God makes connections and sets up unexpected appointments. When we recognize these encounters for what they might be, we can begin to incorporate them into our resets. We can regularly assess what's happened, and think of ways to test those new waters.

You may want to work a reset toward rest into your daily routine. It may be that once a week you take some intentional time to consider what unexpected things God has brought your way. You might want to evaluate your level of joy once a month, or reconsider your work once a year. When we reset, we can acknowledge how we have been pulled off course. It's a chance to be reminded of how we best bear God's image, what it is that floats our boat, and how we can go sailing more often. It's an opportunity to refocus our direction toward the God who created us, knows us best, and offers a better rest.

I've suggested that we could consider the topic of biblical rest as a neighborhood of highly interconnected streets. We've explored how our current conversations about the seventh-day sabbath have prevented many from exploring the rest of the neighborhood. Our new approach to rest will allow us to safely back out of those cul-de-sacs. But there are other dangers that threaten our restful trip through the streets of sabbath.

Cultivating and Keeping Health

Poor health can be a huge distraction from the rest that Christ offers. Exercising stewardship over our physical, emotional, and mental health is one of the most important steps in our journey of rest. While there are always aspects of our health we can't control, it is still our responsibility to treat them as best we can to ensure the most restful journey possible.

At some point in your life, you've probably had a physical ailment that sidelined you for a period of time. When that happens, it's helpful to have someone diagnose what's wrong, suggest treatment for the injury, and set a plan for recovery. This is the process I've experienced for each of my knee injuries. As soon as I realized something was wrong, I scheduled time with a specialist to diagnose the pain, we set a plan to fix it, and I worked the plan as best I could to get back to health as soon as possible.

We are all familiar with that process when it involves caring for our physical health, and a similar process is available for our mental and emotional health. When we recognize that something is out of balance mentally or emotionally, we can seek out people who specialize in those areas, let them help us diagnose what's wrong, and set a plan for treatment. The goal is to always get back to our best functionality as soon as possible so we're not distracted away from the restful journey that Christ has for each of us.

For example, the effects of traumatic experiences on our health can be one of the most dangerous distractions in our journey. While trauma can sideline our mental capabilities and injure us emotionally, the physical results can also be debilitating. While our culture is becoming more aware of the effects of trauma, in many circles it is still not acceptable to admit that, to some degree, we've all been traumatized. Our traumatic injuries may be something in the past, a present reality, or maybe even both. Sometimes the only way to heal is to seek outside help to diagnose the cause and treat it appropriately. The results of trauma don't have to be a dangerous distraction away from rest. When properly treated, it can even become an important and meaningful part of our journey.

Curtis Zackery, author of *Soul Rest*, speaks to the importance of this inner work: "In our culture, it is clear that we value, elevate, and celebrate superficial self-improvement. It seems, though, that inner work has a certain stigma. If someone has adopted a borderline maniacal exercise regime, no one thinks it's out of sorts. But, when someone suggests that they are seeing a counselor or attempting to order their inner world, there is somewhat of a pitying response. . . . We have to fight against the stigma that comes with focusing on our inner well-being so we can find holistic healing."[100]

While some trauma comes in big and dramatic experiences, it can also be handed out in small, bite-sized chunks. Everyone experiences day-to-day activities that over time can build up and drag us down. Without a break from these annoyances, they have the ability to pile up and become another type of distraction. Our jobs can be one common source of these daily stressors. Even if you are in a job you love, one that utilizes your gifts and talents, there are parts of that job that can pile up and become hard to handle. While I love to teach and really enjoy the face-to-face interactions, I find that other parts of that job can sometimes overwhelm me.

In order to regain a proper perspective, one effective treatment for these stressors is to schedule time away from them. This isn't running and hiding from these distractions; it's recognizing that these little things can add up and that a break can, at least temporarily, clean the slate and help us better negotiate our restful journey. We can come back refreshed and ready to enjoy our place to be, and once again answer the call for our thing to do.

How could you establish intentional routines that allow you to treat the different aspects of your physical, mental, and emotional health? Are there things you can build into your daily schedule that will keep your body in physical condition? Do you need weekly conversations with those who can help you unpack your emotional baggage? Would a monthly weekend, away from your stressors, be a good way to regain your focus? What could you do quarterly, or once a year, to make sure your mental health doesn't distract you from who God is calling you to be?

Each of us have the freedom to explore and establish the routines that best cultivate and keep our own health. And since life will continually throw these distractions our direction, your process will need to be revisited regularly.

Separating from Sin

Another danger in our journey is the entanglement of sin. Just like our health, sin can be a roadblock to rest. When we travel down the side street of sin, our ability to experience God's rest is greatly affected.

In chapter 1, we looked at the creation of the cosmos and the unique role that God has given humanity within His creation. We are to rule, subdue, cultivate, and keep. The problem is, we tend to gravitate toward those tasks with our own plan and for our own glory. We sin when we take on that role and attempt to rule without Him. The Bible includes valuable instruction regarding how to avoid this deadly dead end.

In chapter 7, we briefly discussed the first verses of Hebrews 12. Let's consider those words again, but this time in regard to the author's encouragement to believers regarding sin:

Therefore, since we have so great a cloud of witnesses surrounding us, let us also lay aside every encumbrance and the sin which so easily entangles us, and let us run with endurance the race that is set before us, fixing our eyes on Jesus, the author and perfecter of faith, who for the joy set before Him endured the cross, despising the shame, and has sat down at the right hand of the throne of God. For consider Him who has endured such hostility by sinners against Himself, so that you will not grow weary and lose heart. (Hebrews 12:1–3)

There's a lot packed into those three verses, but did you notice what it says about sin? The author encourages us to "lay aside every encumbrance and the sin which so easily entangles us." That's what sin does: it entangles and prevents us from getting about our business. And what's our business? It's ruling and subduing the earth the way God would have us do for His glory.

But let's also notice the first part of the author's instruction. He directs his readers to "lay aside" the sin. The author chose to use the Greek "middle voice" for this action. It signifies that the subject of the sentence (the believer in Christ) participates in the action (laying aside encumbrances and sin). In other words, believers have a responsible role in regard to their separation from sin.

There are several scriptures that similarly describe this process of disentangling from sin (Romans 13:12; Ephesians 4:17–32; Colossians 3:5–11; James 1:21; 1 Peter 2:1). In Ephesians 4:22–24, Paul explains that in the process of laying aside our sin and replacing it with the attributes of Christ, something magical happens to our spirit. We are "renewed," and this renewal is stated in the passive voice, which sounds exactly like what it means: we are passive in that process. It happens to us. Our renewal is not something we do—it's what we receive from God. It's His work in us, and it's what allows us to work with Him in the process. In other words, the way we are able to avoid the dead end of sin is not just by our own efforts to be good. A vital element of this process is that God is renewing who we are, and the way we think, along the way.

It's also important that we invite others into this process with us. When we surround ourselves with those we trust, they can help us see things about ourselves to which we are blind. So today, if you've heard His voice, begin praying for renewal, surround yourself with trustworthy people, and don't be surprised when separating from sin begins to sound unusually attractive.

With a plan in place for maintaining our health, and having constructed space from our sin, we will have the proper perspective to consider the risk of ruts in our road.

Removing Ruts

The last danger we will discuss in the neighborhood of rest is the risk of traveling within dangerous ruts. People are creatures of habit. We love our routines, and they are important for our survival. But the habits that begin as the most helpful of grooves can eventually turn into dangerous ruts in our road. When routines become too ingrained, they can cause us to take our hands off the wheel, not pay attention to the direction we are headed, and potentially miss God's instructions to make a turn in our journey.

In our pursuit of sabbath rest, it is essential to set up routines that help us stay securely hitched to Christ's yoke. These can be daily rituals, weekly habits, or monthly reminders that keep us focused. At times, the obedience Christ encourages is only possible through the creation of such disciplines. And as we've already discussed in this section, the routines we establish can help keep us away from dangerous distractions in the neighborhood. If you meet with others in a small group or as part of a church family, you may have some of these helpful routines already in place. Those settings can be great places to maintain health, separate from sin, and reset back toward rest.

In chapter 5, I suggested that it's sometimes inviting to go back to the repetition of the shadows. I discussed how repetitious routines can become meaningless "checklist items" which are marked off at regular intervals and then forgotten again until the next time they appear on the list. This is one way a good groove can become a distracting rut. If we are to effectively travel in this neighborhood, we can no longer just put our head down and blindly follow a prescribed formula. The routines we need require more pliability than any checklist can offer. When we attach our soul to the one who knows us best, the path will often lead to places we've never been. Our route can change quickly, and listening for God's voice of direction is essential.

Remember the message from Hebrews 3:7: "Therefore, just as the Holy Spirit says, 'Today if you hear His voice . . .'"

When God calls, and that can be any "today" of the week, we need the flexibility to hear Him and respond in step. Grooves allow for these periodic lane changes, but ruts tend to lack this flexibility.

How can we maintain our routines so they don't end up rigid distractions? One helpful tactic is to create intentional obsolescence into your itinerary. This is the idea that we plan, and create the mechanisms necessary for, the regular paving over of any ruts that may develop. Since we are creatures of habit, we sometimes cling to them long after their usefulness is gone. What we need now, and what is good now, is not always the same thing that our past selves needed, or that our future selves will require.

When I worked as a pastor, our staff would often ask the "groove versus rut" questions about our church activities: "Why are we doing what we do? Are we doing this just because it's what we've always done? Is this activity still meeting our needs as a congregation? Is there another groove we could get into that would serve our needs in a better way?" When our staff took time to evaluate what we were doing, we found that some of our events and programs had long ago lost most of their function and purpose. Some of the traditions, usually the ones we were holding on to most tightly, had unknowingly become dangerous distractions. What were once grooves for our church had over time become ruts in our road.

What are the routines you already have to help you experience sabbath rest? Are those activities in line with your new understanding of this topic? When we rethink rest the way we have, it can be an exciting time to reevaluate our long-standing practices to see if they are still helpful for our journey. It may be that we only need a small adjustment—or we may need to start from scratch, repave the road, and find a whole new groove.

Reframing Rest

In the first chapter, we described how much incongruity and confusion the idea of sabbath has within our modern culture. Everyone has a slightly different idea about what sabbath is and how it should be observed. We often need to dig deeper to understand exactly what people mean, and it's common to find that the whole theology has been truncated into just one weekly event.

After this study, we should now realize the weekly sabbath was really only a small part of a much larger theology of rest presented throughout the Old Testament, and that Jesus fulfilled not just one part, but the whole thing. He has invited us as partners into a new covenant. Christ's ministry reframed rest into something new, and our practices should reflect His fulfillment.

Because of all this, we might consider altering the vocabulary we use when speaking about sabbath rest. If people think we are just entering into a cul-de-sac conversation about the seventh day, they will likely miss the breadth and depth of Christ's easy yoke. But when we use new phrases to describe biblical rest, we can begin to leave the confusion behind and invite others to join us on a whole new path.

We've already started to do this to a degree in our culture. We often call an extended break in our routines a "sabbatical." That's a term we've adapted from the text and given a new meaning. When I describe my sabbath experience to others, I've gotten into the habit of using some new categories. You might hear me say something like: "Once a week I celebrate sabbath . . . by seeking out new sweet spots." Statements like this not only remind *me* what Christ's rest is all about, but it also prompts questions from *others* who also need to know. They'll ask, "What did you mean when you said 'sweet spots'?" And that can be an opportunity to help someone else on their path to rethinking rest.

We can also reframe rest by more correctly observing the signs of the new covenant. In chapter 4, we discussed how baptism and communion are signs of our inclusion in Christ's covenant. These signs should be reminders to listen for His voice and follow His direction. We can move baptism back into its rightful place as the sign of an initial faith experience. We can also help transition communion into the meaningful meal it once was by presenting its symbols for all their worth. These are signs of the most important covenant the world has ever known, and we have the opportunity to reframe these meaningful moments back toward rest.

Finally, let's remember that the author of Hebrews suggests there is a sabbath rest that remains for the people of God. It requires us to rest from our works, the same way God did from His. It describes a transition that is monumental in scope and life-changing in practice. So let's be diligent to enter that truth, thrive in the reality of Christ's fulfillment, and more fully experience the rest of our covenant with Jesus.

ACKNOWLEDGMENTS

I began the dive into the topic of biblical rest in my master's program back in 2006. The road from those first ideas to the completion of this project has spanned a significant portion of my life and learning. And there is a "great crowd of witnesses" who have contributed to the process.

It was a professor, Dr. Gary Derickson, who first directed my eye to how Hebrews 3–4 refers back to the Israelites' crisis moments in the wilderness. He also pointed out how grumbling and complaining contributed to their experience of rest. My friend, Dr. Chip Bennett, was the first to suggest I look into Dr. John Walton's work regarding rest. It was Walton's ideas that shifted the foundation of my thesis. As I formulated my ideas into the final project for my doctoral studies, I received valuable input from several professors including, but not limited to, Dr. Karen Jobes, Dr. Warren Gage, Dr. Scott Manor, and Dr. Sam Lamerson.

It took several years, alongside some difficult life circumstances, to convert my doctoral project into the work you find here. I developed an outline from a class I taught at my church and began the writing process. So many people gave valuable feedback along the way. Thanks to my beta readers Rachel Baugh, Brenna Brutcher, Chandler Brutcher, Bob and Lori Cavell, Frank Fleming, Jodi Hall, Lisa Hall, Julie Haupt, Esther Libby, Jerry Morris, Madison Mullen, and Eric Weber. Rachel Baugh is solely responsible for editing out . . . the overabundance of . . . ellipses in my early drafts. Thank God I've been mostly cured of that. . . .

A very special thank you to Dr. John Walton, who responded to the random voice mail I left him in the middle of a pandemic. His scholarship has been a huge influence in the development of my thinking. He was willing to read my manuscript, then offered to work with me on several rounds of edits, encouraged me through the publishing process, and wrote the foreword to this book.

I also could not have finished this project without the encouragement of my wife Lisa. Thanks for sticking with me and giving great feedback, even though I didn't always receive it well. I'm working on that. Love you!

Finally, there are two people who I wish were still around to read this. My dad, Larry, passed away from cancer shortly before my doctoral graduation in 2017. I still resemble him in many ways, and I'm proud to keep his memory alive every time I burp. My big sister and only sibling, Jodi, passed away unexpectedly in her sleep in September of 2020. She and I got our picture taken with Santa for fifty-one straight years and she was my biggest fan. At times she was more excited about this book than I was! I grieve the fact that I can't personally hand these two family members a copy of the finished product.

This book is dedicated to my parents, Larry and Eleanor Hall; to my sister, Jodi; to my wife, Lisa; and to our children, Jacob and Nathaniel. We've seen a little of what the chaos of life can bring. Now, let's all get some rest!

ABOUT THE AUTHOR

Gregory D. Hall is a husband to his high school sweetheart, and father to two twentysomething young men. He hosts the Rethinking Scripture Podcast, where he challenges listeners to rethink what they thought they already knew about the Bible. He's been a college athlete, public school teacher, real estate broker/investor, triathlete, small business owner, pastor, tour leader to Israel, and university professor. This medley of life experiences has meshed nicely with Greg's biblical training (MA in Theological Studies and Doctor of Ministry in Biblical Preaching and Teaching), producing a unique perspective on some of life's most important themes. Greg teaches whenever he can, enjoys swimming laps, and doesn't spend enough time at the Oregon coast.

Greg can be reached through the Contact form at RethinkingScripture.com.

BIBLIOGRAPHY

Allison, Dale C. *The New Moses: A Matthew Typology*. Eugene, OR: Wipf & Stock, 2013.

Augustine of Hippo, "The Confessions of St. Augustin," in *The Confessions and Letters of St. Augustin with a Sketch of His Life and Work*, vol. 1, A Select Library of the Nicene and Post-Nicene Fathers of the Christian Church, First Series, ed. Philip Schaff, trans. J. G. Pilkington. Buffalo, NY: Christian Literature Company, 1886.

Bateman, Herbert W. IV, ed. *Four Views on the Warning Passages in Hebrews*. Grand Rapids, MI: Kregel Academic & Professional, 2007.

Beale, Gregory. K. *The Temple and the Church's Mission: A Biblical Theology of the Dwelling Place of God*. (D. A. Carson, Ed.) (Downers Grove, IL; England: InterVarsity Press; Apollos, 2004).

Bennett, Chip, and Warren Gage. *CS321 Introduction to Plato's Republic: A Christian Reading*. Logos Mobile Education. Bellingham, WA: Lexham Press, 2019.

Brooks, David. *The Second Mountain; the Quest for a Moral Life*. New York: Random House, 2019.

Calvin, John. *Calvin's Commentaries, Vol. 32: Matthew, Mark and Luke, Part II*, trans. John King (1847–50). Comment on Matthew 16:8. https://sacred-texts.com/chr/calvin/cc32/cc32051.htm.

Collins, Jon and Tim Mackie. "Image of God." BibleProject Podcast Series, February/March, 2016. https://bibleproject.com/podcast/series/image-of-god-series.

_____. "161. Two Kinds of Work—7th Day Rest E3." BibleProject Podcast, October, 28, 2019. Podcast, https://bibleproject.com/podcast/two-kinds-work/, 61:00.

_____. "169. Jesus and His Jubilee Mission—7th Day Rest E11." BibleProject Podcast, December 16, 2019. Podcast, https://bibleproject.com/podcast/jesus-and-his-jubilee-mission/, 75:00.

Donato, Christopher J., et al. *Perspectives on the Sabbath*. Nashville: B&H, 2011.

Evans, Rachel H., and J. Chu. *Wholehearted Faith*. San Francisco: Harper One, 2021.

Gage, Warren. A., and L. G. Gage. *The Road to Emmaus: A Walk with a Stranger from Jerusalem*. Fort Lauderdale: St. Andrews House, 2012.

Grant, Adam M. *Think Again: The Power of Knowing What You Don't Know*. New York: Random House, 2021.

Hall, Gregory D. *Beyond the Sabbath's Shadow: A Biblical Understanding and Application of Godly Rest*. DMin Major Project, Knox Seminary, 2017.

Howard, Kevin, and M. Rosenthal. *The Feasts of the Lord: God's Prophetic Calendar from Calvary to the Kingdom*. Nashville: Thomas Nelson, 1997.

Imes, Carmen J. *Bearing God's Name: Why Sinai Still Matters*. Downers Grove, IL: IVP Academic, 2019.

Jobes, Karen H. *Letters to the Church: A Survey of Hebrews and the General Epistles*. Grand Rapids, MI: Zondervan, 2011.

Jobes, Karen H., and Moisès Silva. *Invitation to the Septuagint*. Second Edition. Grand Rapids, MI: Baker Academic, 2015.

Plato. *The Republic of Plato*. Trans. with notes and interpretive essay by Allan Bloom. New York: Basic Books, 1968.

Walton, John H. *Ancient Near Eastern Thought and the Old Testament: Introducing the Conceptual World of the Hebrew Bible*. Grand Rapids, MI: Baker Academic, 2006.

_____. *The Lost World of Genesis One: Ancient Cosmology and the Origins Debate*. Downers Grove, IL: IVP Academic, 2009.

_____. *Genesis*. Grand Rapids, MI: Zondervan, 2001.

_____. *Genesis 1 as Ancient Cosmology*. Winona Lake, IN: Eisenbrauns, 2011.

_____. *The Lost World of Adam and Eve: Genesis 2–3 and the Human Origins Debate*. Downers Grove, IL: IVP Academic, 2015.

_____. *Old Testament Theology for Christians: From Ancient Context to Enduring Belief*. Downers Grove, IL: IVP Academic, 2017.

Walton, John H., T. Longman III, and S. O. Moshier. *The Lost World of the Flood: Mythology, Theology, and the Deluge Debate*. Westmont, IL: InterVarsity Press, 2018.

Walton, John H., and J. Harvey Walton. *The Lost World of the Torah: Law as Covenant and Wisdom in Ancient Context*. Downers Grove, IL: IVP Academic, 2019.

Zackery, Curtis. *Soul Rest: Reclaim Your Life; Return to Sabbath*. A. Stocker, J. Marr, L. Smoyer, & C. Callahan, eds. Bellingham, WA: Kirkdale Press, 2018.

ENDNOTES

Introduction

1 Adam M Grant. *Think Again: The Power of Knowing What You Don't Know.* (New York: Random House, 2021), 4.

2 John H. Walton, *Old Testament Theology for Christians: From Ancient Context to Enduring Belief* (Downers Grove, IL: IVP Academic, 2017), 10.

3 Grant, *Think Again*, 4.

4 Rachel H. Evans and J. Chu, *Wholehearted Faith* (San Francisco: Harper One, 2021), chapter 14.

Chapter 1

5 There was one vacation where this actually happened. I spent most of two whole days lying in a hammock in a resort in Mexico. I lived mostly on chips and salsa.

6 You might not know it, but I'm a bit of a French scholar. I completed two years of French in high school. To this day, I can still count to ten (*un, deux, trois . . .*) at the drop of a chapeau!

7 The seventh-day sabbath commandment is outlined in two different places: first in Exodus 20:8–11 and again in Deuteronomy 5:12–15. One might note that the two versions differ slightly on minor points.

[8] For a more robust view on the history of sabbath observance, I recommend Christopher John Donato, et al., *Perspectives on the Sabbath* (Nashville: B&H, 2011).

[9] This saying has a completely different meaning after the recent pandemic!

[10] It's important to note some confusion around this mention of the Old Testament character of Joshua. Several older English translations (Wycliff, Darby, Geneva, King James) translate this as "Jesus" instead of "Joshua." That's because the names we translate into English as "Jesus" and "Joshua" are actually the same Greek word. A similar situation also occurs in Acts 7:45. I'll discuss this in more detail in Chapter 5.

[11] I acknowledge that there are many different ways people read and understand the events of creation in Genesis 1:1–2:3. Our purpose here is not to try and settle any of those debates. They are great discussions to have, but we are here only to determine the quality and characteristics of the "rest" that God experienced.

[12] In my days as a youth pastor, I would have paused on this point just long enough to make everyone a little uncomfortable. Feel free to sit here for as long as you need.

[13] I like the term vicegerent (vice-jir-ent) over "vice-regent" or even "coregent." I believe it to be a more accurate descriptor of the relationship God originally set up with humanity. A "vicegerent" is the official administrative deputy of a ruler or head of state. It is comprised of *vice* (Latin for "in place of") and *gerere* (Latin for "to carry on, conduct"). This suggests that God is still present in the process, but has delegated a portion of His rule and authority to humanity.

[14] I'm borrowing much of the descriptive language in this section from the work of Dr. John H. Walton, who presents a much more scholarly account of these concepts in several places including, but not limited to *Ancient Near Eastern Thought and the Old Testament: Introducing*

the Conceptual World of the Hebrew Bible (Grand Rapids, MI: Baker Academic, 2006); *The Lost World of Genesis One: Ancient Cosmology and the Origins Debate.* (Downers Grove, IL: IVP Academic, 2009); and *Genesis 1 as Ancient Cosmology* (Winona Lake, IN: Eisenbrauns, 2011).

[15] It's on this point that the Bible's story of creation is dramatically different than seemingly similar extrabiblical stories. The Bible states that there is only one God that rules everything. There is no competition. In its day, this was a radical idea for those that held a pluralistic worldview. The biblical author uses this contrast to discount the pagan, polytheistic versions of creation.

[16] Maybe the most often-referenced of these stories is the Enuma Elish, a Babylonian creation myth that tells how the god Marduk rested (ruled) from a temple once the cosmos was established and ordered. For more see "Proposition 7, Divine Rest Is in a Temple," in Walton, *The Lost World of Genesis One*, 71.

[17] Here is Walton's longer statement for more context: "The difference is the piece of information that everyone knew in the ancient world and to which most modern readers are totally oblivious: Deity rests in a temple, and only in a temple. This is what temples were built for. We might even say that this is what a temple is—a place for divine rest. Perhaps even more significant, in some texts the construction of a temple is associated with cosmic creation. What does divine rest entail? Most of us think of rest as disengagement from the cares, worries and tasks of life. What comes to mind is sleeping in or taking an afternoon nap. But in the ancient world rest is what results when a crisis has been resolved or when stability has been achieved, when things have 'settled down.' Consequently, normal routines can be established and enjoyed. For deity this means that the normal operations of the cosmos can be undertaken. This is more a matter of engagement without obstacles rather than disengagement without responsibilities." Walton, *The Lost World of Genesis One*, 71–72.

[18] As Dr. Gregory Beale points out, "The prophet Ezekiel portrays Eden as being on a mountain (Ezek. 28:14, 16). Israel's temple was on Mount Zion (e.g., Exod. 15:17), and the end-time temple was to be located on a mountain (Ezek. 40:2; 43:12; Rev. 21:10)." G. K. Beale, *The Temple and the Church's Mission: A Biblical Theology of the Dwelling Place of God*, vol. 17, D. A. Carson, ed. (Downers Grove, IL; England: InterVarsity Press; Apollos, 2004), 73.

[19] Several authors see this choice of words as theologically significant. According to Beale, "There may also be significance that the word used for God 'putting' Adam 'into the garden' in Genesis 2:15 is not the usual Hebrew word for 'put' (*sûm*) but is the word typically translated as 'to rest' (*nûaḥ*). The selection of a word with overtones of 'rest' may indicate that Adam was to begin to reflect the sovereign rest of God." Beale, *The Temple and the Church's Mission*. vol. 17, 69–70.

[20] Jon Collins and Dr. Tim Mackie discuss this use of *nuakh* in more detail in the BibleProject Podcast's Seventh-Day Rest series, episode 3. There are fourteen episodes in this series. Every episode is worthy of close study. Jon Collins and Tim Mackie, "161. Two Kinds of Work – 7th Day Rest E3," BibleProject Podcast, October 28, 2019, 61:00, https://bibleproject.com/podcast/two-kinds-work.

[21] Walton suggests that the garden of Eden is best understood as the center of sacred space, the first temple. He proposes Adam and Eve were more than just gardeners, they were filling priestly roles in sacred space. Walton says it this way: "the point of caring for sacred space should be seen as much more than landscaping or even priestly duties. Maintaining order made one a participant with God in the ongoing task of sustaining the equilibrium God had established in the cosmos." John H. Walton, *The Lost World of Adam and Eve: Genesis 2–3 and the Human Origins Debate* (Downers Grove, IL: IVP Academic, 2015), 107.

[22] By the way, the carts at IKEA are amazing. All four wheels independently pivot 360 degrees. In the "world of carts," their maneuverability is unmatched.

[23] Dr. Carmen Joy Imes discusses several examples of liminality, some including sociological applications. She suggests liminality not only exists in doorways but also airports, wedding ceremonies, pregnancies, and colleges. According to Imes, "Few people actually enjoy liminality. We have an inborn desire to seek order and belonging and predictability." Carmen J. Imes, *Bearing God's Name: Why Sinai Still Matters* (Downers Grove, IL: IVP Academic, 2019), 17.

[24] John H. Walton and J. Harvey Walton, *The Lost World of the Torah: Law as Covenant and Wisdom in Ancient Context* (Downers Grove, IL: IVP Academic, 2019), 113.

[25] Beale, *The Temple and the Church's Mission*, vol. 17, 81–82.

[26] A point emphasized by these comments from Walton, "In verses 17–19 we are again faced with a curse, this time directed at the ground. What does it mean for the ground to be cursed? The verbal root used here ('rr) is recognized as the opposite of bless (brk). To bless someone is to put that person under God's protection, enjoying God's favor. To curse is to remove from God's protection and favor. It does not mean putting a hex on something or changing its character or nature by magical or mystical means. It does not mean to bewitch or put a spell on something. . . . As a result of the ground being removed from God's favor, protection, and blessing, it will yield its produce only through hard labor. . . . The impact of this curse is that, though food is still made available to people, it will be much harder to produce it." John H. Walton, *Genesis* (Grand Rapids, MI: Zondervan, 2001), 229.

[27] The same Hebrew word is used to describe Eve's "pain" in childbirth and Adam's "toil" eating from the land. English versions often choose to translate them differently, but they are the same Hebrew word. According to Walton, "The noun translated, "pain," in the first line is . . . a word used only two other times in the Old Testament (Gen. 3:17; 5:29). Nouns from the same root . . . refer to pain, agony, hardship, worry, nuisance, and anxiety. The verbal root . . . occurs in a wide range of stems

with a semantic range that primarily expresses grief and worry. What is important to note about this profile is that the root is not typically used to target physical pain, but mental or psychological anguish (though physical pain may accompany or be the root cause of the anguish). Walton, *Genesis*, 227.

[28] I give credit for this perspective to Dr. Gib Binnington, who taught a class for teachers called "Disrupting the Disruptor."

[29] A point emphasized in these two passages: "Thus says the LORD: Heaven is my throne, and the earth is my footstool; what is the house that you would build for me, and what is the place of my rest?" (Isaiah 66:1); and "For the LORD has chosen Zion; He has desired it for His habitation. This is My resting place forever; here I will dwell, for I have desired it" (Psalm 132:13–14). God's restful rule is conducted in a throne room, which includes heaven and extends to the footstool of His earthly temple.

[30] John H. Walton, *Old Testament Theology for Christians: From Ancient Context to Enduring Belief* (Downers Grove, IL: IVP Academic, 2017), 171.

Chapter 2

[31] When I teach, I usually prefer 1980s movie references. I was so close with this one!

[32] I'm borrowing the use of "hyperlink" not only from the internet, but also from Jon Collins and Dr. Tim Mackie of BibleProject. They often use this term to suggest an intended connection between otherwise seemingly unrelated biblical texts and ideas.

[33] The biblical text actually describes the body of water that consumes Pharaoh as the "sea of reeds." Maps that suggest a path for the exodus are quite varied on its location. Some don't show the people crossing any water because scholars have not reached consensus about its location.

[34] The curse in Genesis 3:17 was placed on the land, not the people. This important distinction is highlighted by Walton: (see endnote 26).

[35] There seems to be a theme within Scripture where God deals more harshly with the initial lawbreakers, to show the gravity of the situation and to be an example for others. In Joshua 6–7, Achan and his family are exposed as the first breakers of the covenant within the conquest of the Promised Land. He and his (likely complicit) family are stoned, burned, and then covered with rocks (the same fate as the enemies of Israel in Jericho). In Acts 5, Ananias and Sapphira were the first to break from the new covenant after Pentecost. They both fell dead for lying to the Holy Spirit.

[36] Since these three feasts happen in rapid succession, sometimes all three are referred to by only mentioning the first, "Passover" (Luke 2:41; John 2:13; 6:4; 11:55); but at other times more detail is given (Mark 14:1; Luke 22:1).

[37] These feasts were linked back to the story of the exodus from slavery, which ultimately is a picture of the Israelites' attempt to return to the function and order of the original creation.

[38] Sabbath rest for the land only applied to the land inside Israel's borders. It didn't apply to Jewish-owned land in foreign lands. According to Deuteronomy 15:3, the release of debts had similar restrictions. Loans to foreigners were not required to be released. These boundaries were just another reminder of Eden. A certain set of rules existed within its boundaries, but a different standard existed outside those borders.

[39] This description is not a foreshadowing literary device. We literally got married at night, in the middle of a snow and ice storm!

[40] John H. Walton, T. Longman III, and S. O. Moshier, *The Lost World of the Flood: Mythology, Theology, and the Deluge Debate* (Westmont, IL: InterVarsity Press, 2018), 106.

[41] There are even questions about who the subject was. The painter was never able to figure out more than just his name. The painting is called *James Hunter Black Draftee* (1965).

[42] This is a very platonic way of viewing God's end goal. We will discuss some of Plato's ideas in chapter 3, including his "world of the forms," that have contributed to the idea that our final resting place will be in the heavens, instead of the new earth.

Chapter 3

[43] Augustine of Hippo, "The Confessions of St. Augustin," in *The Confessions and Letters of St. Augustin with a Sketch of His Life and Work*, vol. 1, A Select Library of the Nicene and Post-Nicene Fathers of the Christian Church, First Series, ed. Philip Schaff, trans. J. G. Pilkington (Buffalo, NY: Christian Literature Company, 1886), 45.

[44] Some of the concepts and examples in this section were inspired by the BibleProject Podcast series *Image of God*. In that series, Collins and Mackie discuss many other aspects and intricacies of image bearing not mentioned here. Jon Collins and Tim Mackie, *Image of God*, BibleProject Podcast Series, February/March 2016, https://bibleproject.com/podcast/series/image-of-god-series.

[45] Sometimes this presents itself in the suggestion that the Law must be segmented into three categories: civil laws, ceremonial laws, and moral laws. It's often thought that the civil and ceremonial aspects of the Mosaic Law shouldn't apply to New Testament believers, but that the moral aspects of the Law should apply today. While these are good discussions to have, understanding the Mosaic Law in this way encourages people to approach the text compartmentally. It dramatically decreases a reader's ability to study the interconnected themes of the entire biblical text (Old and New Testaments).

[46] I still remember the revelation I experienced when the Old Testament practice of animal sacrifice was connected to Jesus's role as the Lamb (one of the Old Testament sacrificial animals) of God.

[47] According to Howard and Rosenthal, "Yom Kippur was designated by the Lord as a day in which 'you shall afflict your souls' (Lev 23:27, 32). By definition this was understood to mean fasting (cf. Ezra 8:21). It was a day devoted to fasting and repenting of one's sins during the past year. The Israelite who failed to devote himself to fasting and repentance on Yom Kippur was to be 'cut off from his people' (Lev. 23:29). Yom Kippur was also a day with prohibitions against all forms of work." Kevin Howard and Marvin Rosenthal. *The Feasts of the Lord: God's Prophetic Calendar from Calvary to the Kingdom* (Nashville: Thomas Nelson, 1997), 120.

[48] Interestingly, at least one time this goat wandered back into camp . . . which really ruined the picture that they were trying to paint. Can you imagine seeing all your sins literally walking back into town? They eventually changed the custom and began shoving the scapegoat down a steep mountain to ensure its death.

[49] In John 1:29, John the Baptist sees Jesus and says to those who were with him, "Behold, the Lamb of God who takes away the sins of the world!" This idea of "taking away sins" is a hyperlink back to the scapegoat on the Day of Atonement.

[50] These points are illustrated as a chiasmus, a common way authors of Greek literature structured their writing. It follows a pattern where parallel elements correspond in an inverted order (i.e., A-B-C-C'-B'-A', usually with the author's main point placed in the center position (in the example the letters C and C' are in the center). I often look for creative ways to display this ancient structure. For some of my Bible studies, my weekly choice of shirts followed a chiastic pattern. I know, I need some help.

[51] Many of the ideas presented in this section come from Dr. Chip Bennett and Dr. Warren Gage's Christian understanding of Greek philosophic ideas and Plato's *Republic*. I recommend the following resource for those interested in understanding more about philosophy's influence on the way the gospel was originally communicated in a Roman world: Chip

Bennett and Warren Gage, CS321 *Introduction to Plato's Republic: A Christian Reading*, Logos Mobile Education (Bellingham, WA: Lexham Press, 2019).

[52] If you've taken a philosophy class, you might have studied this. It is possibly the most famous of Plato's examples and is found in Book VII of *The Republic*.

[53] That is, at least since the Tower of Babel events discussed in Genesis 11:1–9.

[54] This is not limited to the idea of shadows and forms. Another well-known example is found in the first chapter of John's gospel. The disciple begins his gospel with this statement: "In the beginning was the Logos (Greek for "Word"), and the Logos was with God, and the Logos was God." Later in the same chapter he writes, "And the Logos became flesh and tabernacled among us" (John 1:14). Plato and other philosophers had previously discussed the existence of a nonphysical divine reason implicit in the cosmos which gives it order, form, and meaning. The title they gave this philosophic concept was the *Logos* (which in Greek can mean "word," "reason," or "plan"). In the introduction to John's gospel, he uses this well-established philosophic idea of the Logos and combines it with language that mimics the Jewish creation account ("In the beginning") to describe Jesus, the Logos who came from the unseen realm, became flesh, and tabernacles among humanity. John's ability to set this multicultural hook early in His gospel most certainly contributed to the spread of the gospel in the first-century Hellenistic world.

[55] Plato, *The Republic of Plato*, trans. with notes and interpretive essay by Allan Bloom (New York: Basic Books, 1968), 199.

[56] Plato suggested there could be someone who was completely righteous or "just." He also concluded that such a "just man" would end up being "whipped; he'll be racked; he'll be bound; he'll have both of his eyes burned out; and, at the end, when he has undergone every sort of evil, he'll be crucified." Plato, *The Republic*, 39.

Chapter 4

[57] Thanks to Dr. Leah Payne for providing this analogy, which highlights the significance of this cultural phenomenon.

[58] Movies like *Lucas* (1986) and *Can't Buy Me Love* (1987) featured the slow clap. As a result, these types of scenes were also masterfully mocked in the 2001 spoof *Not Another Teen Movie*.

[59] Matthew leads all other gospel writers by mentioning the "fulfillment" of prophecy fourteen times (Matthew 1:22; 2:15, 17, 23; 3:15; 4:14; 5:17; 8:17; 12:17; 13:35; 21:4; 26:54, 56; and 27:9).

[60] The Hebrew Bible is referred to as the TaNaKh, which is an acronym made from these three main sections into which the Hebrew scriptures are organized. The "T" stands for Torah, which refers to the first five books. This section is also referred to as the Law (of Moses). The N refers to Nevi'im, the Hebrew word for Prophets. The K represents the Ketuvim, which means "Writings" and contains the Psalms, other poetry, and some random other books that didn't fit into the first two groupings. This is the organization to which Jesus is referring when He describes the Scriptures as the "Law and Prophets and Psalms."

[61] There are at least two other things going on in this passage that are worthy of mention.

First, according to Mackie of the Bible Project, Jesus seems to insert an extra line, from Isaiah 58:6, into His quote of Isaiah 61. The line from chapter 58, "To set free those who are oppressed," is in the context of the seventh-day sabbath. Mackie suggests that by combining this seventh-day sabbath context (Isaiah 58) with the Jubilee passage (Isaiah 61), Jesus is suggesting those two passages are really talking about the same thing: the ministry of rest that Jesus has come to fulfill. Jon Collins and Tim Mackie, "169. Jesus and His Jubilee Mission – 7th Day Rest E11," BibleProject Podcast, December 16, 2019, 75:00, https://bibleproject. com/podcast/jesus-and-his-jubilee-mission.

Second, Jesus seems to end His Scripture reading in the middle of a sentence. Isaiah 61:2 reads, "To proclaim the favorable year of the LORD and the day of vengeance of our God." Jesus quotes the language regarding the "favorable year of the LORD," but then stops and does not mention the "day of vengeance of our God" that concludes the sentence in Isaiah. It may be that Jesus fulfilled the "favorable year of the LORD" ministry in His first coming, and that the "day of vengeance of our God" could refer to events associated with another time.

[62] This verb, in the Greek manuscripts, is in the perfect tense, which means Jesus's fulfillment is a past completed action which has ongoing present implications. Here, at the very beginning of His public ministry, Jesus is saying that He has already fulfilled the ultimate Jubilee.

[63] Jesus also speaks to this fulfillment in Matthew 11:2–6 when John the Baptist sends messengers to Jesus asking if he is the One they have come to expect from the Old Testament prophecies. Jesus sends word back to John from this same Isaiah passage. They report to John that the sick and lame are being brought back to full functionality and "the poor have the gospel preached to them" (Matthew 11:5).

[64] Some more recent studies have suggested that people don't necessarily learn best by emphasizing one preferred learning style. So, the early theories about learning styles are probably not as accurate as researchers once thought. It turns out that people likely learn best by employing a variety of styles into their study habits.

[65] Consider Paul's description of this situation in his letter to the Galatians. He suggests Christ's ministry is to set humanity free from the yoke of slavery to sin: "It was for freedom that Christ set us free; therefore, keep standing firm and do not be subject again to a yoke of slavery" (Galatians 5:1). But freedom from that yoke only allows someone to be attached to another. This choice between "two yokes" is the same message we saw in Jeremiah. Humanity is always yoked to something—either the rule of slavery to sin, or to the rule of God.

66 There were provisions within God's revelation that ensured that the roles of the king and the priest would remain separate. The priests were only from the tribe of Levi, while the kingly line (first from Saul's tribe of Benjamin) would eventually follow David's line from within the tribe of Judah.

67 Carmen J. Imes, *Bearing God's Name: Why Sinai Still Matters* (Downers Grove, IL: IVP Academic, 2019), 145.

68 The gospel of John supports this claim many times: first, by telling us that, during his earthly ministry, Jesus "tabernacled" among us (John 1:14). Jesus further downplays the ministry of the temple in Jerusalem when He tells a woman at a well in Samaria, "an hour is coming when neither in this mountain nor in Jerusalem will you worship the Father" (John 4:21).

69 Let's remember the connection Jesus has with the creation event (see John 1:1–3).

70 By stating this, I don't claim to understand what it is that sheep are supposed to do.

71 The Greek word describing the man's hand literally means "dry"—like a dry and withered plant.

72 A truth found not only in Scripture, but also in junior high English classes across the country!

Chapter 5

73 Interestingly, there are three times Ἰησοῦς is translated as "Lord" for sake of translational clarity (Luke 10:39; John 4:1; Jude 5).

74 Dr. Karen H. Jobes is one of the best of the current scholars in this field of study. I'd like to thank her for her time, expertise, and willingness to personally explain many of the nuances found in Hebrews 3–4. For a good introduction to Septuagint studies, one should read Karen

H. Jobes and Moisès Silva. *Invitation to the Septuagint,* second edition (Grand Rapids, MI: Baker Academic, 2015).

[75] Karen H. Jobes, *Letters to the Church: A Survey of Hebrews and the General Epistles* (Zondervan, 2011), 67.

[76] I've unpacked some of the linguistic nuances at play between Hebrews 3–4, Psalm 95, and Exodus 17 in my doctoral project, *Beyond the Sabbath's Shadow: A Biblical Understanding and Application of Godly Rest.* If you are interested in that sort of study, a copy is available at RethinkingRest. com. You could be one of the few people to ever lay eyes on that project! The list includes a handful of professors, my family, and a guy at my church named Frank!

[77] Cross-references are really helpful links to related Scripture passages that some printed Bibles include (either in the middle column or sometimes at the bottom of the page). An online search for "Bible cross-references" will suggest several free electronic options of the same.

[78] As the fictitious news anchor, Ron Burgundy, might say.

Chapter 6

[79] The events in the beginning of Exodus are much more interesting than going through a class syllabus. I'll never forget the first time I taught a "pandemic class" with students over video conferencing. As I was making my way through the class syllabus, one of the students said, very loudly, "This class is sooo boring! All he's doing is reading through the syllabus." One of my students had forgotten to mute her microphone, walked away from her computer, and begun talking to her roommate. Unfortunately, her assessment was accurate! That particular class was terribly boring.

[80] This point was first introduced to me by my professor Dr. Gary Derickson. It was in his class that I began my exploration into the topic of biblical rest.

[81] This reminds me of another story. In 1 Kings 17–19 Elijah has a showdown with several hundred prophets of pagan gods. After the Lord comes through in big and dramatic ways, Elijah fears for his life and flees the entire length of the land. He ultimately ends up severely depressed and in a cave on Mt. Sinai. He listens for God's voice in the loudness of the strong wind, a massive earthquake, and a raging fire, but the Lord's message was not in any of those. Then the text says there was "a sound of a gentle blowing" (1 Kings 19:12). The King James Version translated it as the more familiar "a still small voice." Literally, the Hebrew words are "voice," "silence," and "thin"—or, a voice of thin silence. One of my tour guides in Israel, Dr. Halvor Ronning of the Home for Bible Translators and Scholars in Jerusalem, explained it like this: "If we had been there in the cave with a tape recorder, it would have just been silent." Dr. Ronning said this story introduced the idea of "thin silence." In an utterly silent moment when Elijah is absolutely desperate and wishing he could die, it says the silence got "thin." Somehow God's presence was there in the silence and penetrated the silence. It was so powerful that Elijah got up out of his despair and was able to continue his ministry. Halvor Ronning, personal communication, 2006.

[82] It's likely that this water was more than just bitter to the taste. This description is likely a warning that the water would cause one to get sick, or possibly even kill those who consumed it. That would certainly leave a bitter taste in one's mouth!

[83] According to Dr. Warren Gage, this story is one of many third-day references in the Old Testament that prefigure the resurrection of Jesus. He suggests that, like Jesus's story, there are several stories in the Old Testament where someone survives a "death-like experience" on the third day. This story in Exodus 15 may have been one of the stories Jesus recounted to the disciples on the road to Emmaus (Luke 24:13–35). W. A. Gage and L. G. Gage, *The Road to Emmaus: A Walk with a Stranger from Jerusalem* (Fort Lauderdale: St. Andrews House, 2012). Dr. Gage has also depicted several of these stories in professionally animated short videos at www.WatermarkGospel.com.

[84] This reminds me of Job's story in the Old Testament. Job lost everything he owned and his entire family died. Through this process Job is conflicted and he asks God for an answer for why he is being treated this way. Then God gives a lengthy response (Job 38:1–42:2) where He explains the complexity of the organization of the cosmos. From Job's point of view, things seem unjust, but from God's perspective Job is a small part of complex creation and there is no way he can understand how everything works with his limited view. What's Job's answer? "I have declared that which I did not understand, things too wonderful for me, which I did not know" (Job 42:3).

[85] This name was transliterated from the Hebrew word of the same sound. It has nothing to do with the English meaning of sin. It's just a place name. The mountain in this area (Sinai) is a deviation of the same.

[86] Some see the Israelites' decision at Kadesh Barnea, when they sent the twelve spies into the land, as the event that prevented their entrance. But the decision made at Kadesh Barnea was reflective of the hardness they first developed at Meribah and Massah, the first time they tested God.

[87] Some commentators try to lump the two episodes together and explain them as the same event.

[88] These stories are mentioned in each of the synoptic gospels (Matthew, Mark, and Luke). Those gospels are called "synoptic" because the majority of their content is similar (like the English word "synonym"). In contrast, the fourth gospel (John) contains largely different content.

[89] Examples of "Moses typology" are seen throughout the New Testament. Complete works have been written suggesting a pervasive attempt by the New Testament authors (and the early church) to connect the ministries of Moses and Jesus. In his work, Allison summarizes the typology this way: "of all the Jewish figures with whom Jesus is implicitly or explicitly compared in Christian literature of the first few centuries, Moses, both in terms of frequency and significance, holds pride of place." Dale C. Allison, *The New Moses: A Matthew Typology* (Eugene, OR: Wipf & Stock, 2013).

90 This is also a link back to the forty days and nights of fasting that Moses experienced on Mt. Sinai (Exodus 34:28).

91 Luke 4:2 says that Jesus was "tempted by the devil." A more literal translation would say He was "put to the test by the devil." Does that sound familiar at all? Maybe it brings the story of Adam and Eve to mind? They too were tested by the devil in a garden. But they failed the test, and were removed from God's rest.

92 To further clarify between the two Meribah events, the Bible sometimes describes the episode from Numbers 20 as "Meribah-kadesh, in the wilderness of Zin" (Numbers 27:14; Deuteronomy 32:51).

Chapter 7

93 Here is the larger quote where Calvin discusses the disciples' response to Jesus's miraculous feeding of the thousands: "And certainly, it was shameful ingratitude that, after having seen bread created out of nothing, and in such abundance as to satisfy many thousands of men, and after having seen this done twice, they are now anxious about bread, as if their Master did not always possess the same power. From these words we infer that all who have once or twice experienced the power of God, and distrust it for the future are convinced of unbelief; for it is faith that cherishes in our hearts the remembrance of the gifts of God, and faith must have been laid asleep, if we allow them to be forgotten. John Calvin, *Calvin's Commentaries, vol. 32: Matthew, Mark and Luke, Part II*, trans. John King (1847–50), Comment on Matthew 16:8, https://sacred-texts.com/chr/calvin/cc32/cc32051.htm.

94 Yes, this is a nod to Liam Neeson's character in the movie *Taken*.

95 David Brooks, *The Second Mountain: The Quest for a Moral Life* (New York: Random House, 2019), 89–93.

96 Bob Goff, Twitter, March 20, 2021, https://twitter.com/bobgoff/status/1373478395330273283?lang=en.

[97] There have been many debates about how to properly understand and apply the "warning passages" found in Hebrews 2:1–4; 4:12–13; 6:4–8; and 10:26–31. Are these warnings given to true believers, nonbelievers, or some combination of the two? For a good historical perspective, I would suggest reading H. W. Bateman IV, ed., *Four Views on the Warning Passages in Hebrews* (Grand Rapids, MI: Kregel Academic & Professional, 2007).

[98] According to Dr. Gary W. Derickson, "In the book of Numbers (after Kadish-Barneia) God does not desert Israel. Chapter fourteen is followed by chapter fifteen. God encouraged the Israelites to teach their children about the sacrifices that they would perform in the promised land. He continued to provide for the Israelites in the wilderness. God gave them covering and food up until the day they entered the promised land. The author is not talking about losing their salvation . . . just their rest." Gary W. Derickson, "The Book of Hebrews," New Testament Survey (class lecture, Oregon Theological Seminary, 2006).

[99] I realize that this comparison places Tacoma, Washington, as the symbolic equivalent of Egypt. Let me just say, Tacoma really was a great place to live!

Afterword

[100] Curtis Zackery, *Soul Rest: Reclaim Your Life; Return to Sabbath*, eds. A. Stocker, J. Marr, L. Smoyer, and C. Callahan (Bellingham, WA: Kirkdale Press, 2018), 31.